WRITING A REPORT

HOW TO PREPARE, WRITE & PRESENT REALLY EFFECTIVE REPORTS

JOHN BOWDEN

howtobooks

For Paula, Forever.

Published by How To Books Ltd
Spring Hill House, Spring Hill Road
Begbroke, Oxford OX5 1RX, United Kingdom
Tel: (01865) 375794. Fax: (01865) 370162
info@howtobooks.co.uk
www.howtobooks.co.uk

How To Books greatly reduce the carbon footprint of their books
by sourcing their typesetting and printing in the UK.

First edition 1991
Second edition 1994
Third edition 1996
Fourth edition 1997
Fifth edition 2000
Sixth edition 2002
Seventh edition 2004
Eighth edition 2008
Reprinted 2009
Ninth edition 2011

British Library Cataloguing in Publication Data
A catalogue record for this book is available from
the British Library.

ISBN 978 1 84528 470 1

Cover design by Baseline Arts Ltd, Oxford
Produced for How To Books by Deer Park Productions, Tavistock
Typeset by Kestrel Data, Exeter
Printed and bound by Bell & Bain Ltd, Glasgow

NOTE: The material in this book is set out in good faith for general
guidance and no liability can be accepted for loss or expense
incurred as a result of relying in particular circumstances on
statements made in the book. Laws and regulations are complex and
liable to change, and readers should check the current position with
the relevant authorities before making personal arrangements.

Contents

List of Illustrations

Preface
to the ninth edition

Report writing can be described as a career skill. It is a task which has become increasingly associated not only with academic assignments, but also with a wide range of jobs and occupations. Today, good communication skills and the ability to write effective reports are essential competencies for every successful student and business person.

Now in its ninth edition, this extensively revised and updated handbook explains how you can write reports that will be:

♦   read without unnecessary delay;

♦   understood without undue effort;

♦   accepted and, where applicable, acted upon.

To achieve these aims you must do more than present all the relevant facts accurately; you must communicate in a way that is both *acceptable* and *intelligible* to your readers.

The book is divided into three parts. Part 1 describes the systematic approach needed to produce an effective report, regardless of the subject-matter. It takes you step-by-step all the way from being asked to write a report to issuing a tailor-made product which meets the needs of all your readers.

In Part 2 we turn to the creative side of writing. Producing a professional report today requires the merging of the technologies of communication, computers and graphic design. What you say is important. But how you say it and how it looks are crucial in creating a high-impact report that stands out from the deluge of material your audience inevitably receives.

Part 3 describes some common types of report in more detail. This section complements Parts 1 and 2 by highlighting the particular emphases associated with each report type.

With this book at hand, you can consistently produce high-impact, professional reports that not only inform, but also guide and influence your readers. In today's communication age, that is an achievement not to be undervalued.

John Bowden

Acknowledgements

Many people assisted in the production of this book and I am grateful to them all. I would particularly like to thank Mrs Nicky Jayesinghe, Head of Science and Education at the British Medical Association, for her kind permission to reproduce various items from reports produced under the auspices of the BMA Board of Science, at Appendix 2, as examples of current best practice.

Part One

The Practical Side of Report Writing

1
Preparation and Planning

To fail to prepare is to prepare to fail. The importance of preparation and planning cannot be stressed too highly. Often, however, writers simply ignore this aspect or dismiss it as too mechanical to be worthwhile. As a result they plough too quickly into the writing process itself and end up failing to realise their full potential. Anything you commit to paper before your overall plan has taken shape is likely to be wasted; it will be like a bricklayer starting to build the wall of a house before the architect has drawn up the plans.

Before you write a single word you must:

♦ Set your objective.

♦ Assess your readership.

♦ Decide what information you will need.

♦ Prepare your skeletal framework.

♦ Test and revise your skeletal framework.

Collectively these activities constitute the planning stage of report writing, and the amount of time and thought you spend on them will make a *vast* difference to the effectiveness of all the work that will follow, by:

♦ continually reminding you of your overall objective

♦ making you constantly 'think readers'

◆ ensuring you know what information you will need to gather

◆ giving you clear guidelines to follow when writing each section

◆ enabling you to rise above the detail and obtain an overview of the entire report at any time.

SETTING YOUR OBJECTIVE

It is essential to establish your precise objective. You must first be absolutely sure of the purpose of your report. Only then can you even begin to think about *what* you are going to write and *how* you are going to write it.

A clearly defined objective has a number of important benefits:

◆ It helps you decide what information to include – and leave out.

◆ It helps you pitch the report at the right level.

◆ It makes it easier to write the report.

Only by continually thinking about your objective – or **Terms of Reference** – can you expect to remain relevant throughout and ensure that everything that *should* be covered *has* been covered – and that everything that *should not* be covered *has not* been.

An objective is not what you intend to **write**, it is what you intend to **achieve**. Writing a research report is not an objective, it is a *task*. The *objective* is to extend the readers' knowledge of the world by reducing their uncertainty and increasing their understanding of it. Writing a trouble-shooting report is not an objective, it is a *task*. The *objective* is to locate the cause of some problem and then suggest ways to remove or treat it. Concentrate on the **objective**, not the associated task.

So what do you want to achieve? What **results** are you hoping for? What do you want to happen next? Only when you have identified this 'bottom line' can you begin to concentrate on getting your message across effectively.

Here are some possible overall objectives for a report writer:

♦   to inform

♦   to describe

♦   to explain

♦   to instruct

♦   to evaluate (and recommend)

♦   to provoke debate

♦   to persuade.

So far, so good. But an objective to inform, describe or explain is too general. You need to be more specific. Perhaps it is to inform sales staff of the details of the new commission scheme. The more closely you can identify your precise objective – preferably in just one sentence – the more useful your report is likely to be.

There is a great advantage in setting a clear objective. If the report has been commissioned, you can go back to the person who requested it and ask them to have a look at your objective to make sure they agree with it. If they don't, find out *precisely* what they *do* expect from you. By taking just a few minutes to clear this up at the earliest realistic time, you will avoid the very real risk of wasting days, weeks or even months on unnecessary and irrelevant work.

ASSESSING YOUR READERSHIP

The next stage is to identify and assess your readership. In many cases, you know who will be reading your report and the detailed content, style and structure can then be matched to their level of knowledge and expertise:

♦ Concentrate on points they will care about.

♦ Explain things they do not know.

♦ Address questions and concerns they would be likely to raise.

Often, however, you do *not* know your readers personally. Try to find out something about them. The following questions will prove useful:

♦ Are the readers alike or mixed?

♦ Are they used to reading and understanding reports?

♦ How much time will they spend on this report?

♦ What do they already know?

♦ What else will they need to know?

Obviously there are many other questions you may wish to ask. However, finding the answers to these five will always provide an excellent start to your target audience research. It is essential that you have a clear understanding of your readership while creating the report so as to focus on *their* needs and expectations. A report which is perceived as reader-friendly will always go down better than one that is introspective.

DECIDING WHAT INFORMATION YOU WILL NEED

For some reports, you will need to collect very little information, while for others you will require a great deal. You will need to think this through carefully, either on your own or with other people.

It is often useful to discuss this with the person who commissioned the report and with prospective readers, particularly any key decision makers. Are there any specific areas they would like covered? The very fact that people have been consulted at this early stage will involve them and, psychologically, this will greatly increase the likelihood of them accepting your conclusions and any recommendations you may make.

You have already written down your specific objective. Take another look at it and see what it tells you. For example, if you were asked to investigate the circumstances surrounding an accident in a canteen kitchen, your objective could be agreed to be: *To investigate how an employee received injuries from a food mixer whilst working in the canteen.* You will now draw up a general list of areas you will need to cover:

◆   What happened?

◆   What were the consequences?

◆   Was the employee properly trained?

◆   Was the machine properly maintained?

◆   Was it avoidable?

Consider everything, and later check it against your objective to make sure it is relevant. Once you have done this you can start to list specific questions that will need to be answered. For example, under *Was the machine properly maintained?* supplementary information you might require would include:

♦   Was a full service record maintained?

♦   Was the machine in good working order?

♦   Have any other problems been reported?

You can draw up your lists of general areas to be covered and specific questions that will need to be asked in any way you like. There are no rules. Use whatever method suits you best. Many writers mind map the information they will need to obtain.

Rather than starting at the top of the page and working down in sentences, lists or words, you begin at the *centre* with the overall topic of your report – and branch out as your information requirements become readily apparent (see Figure 1).

Mind mapping your total research needs has a number of significant advantages over relying on experience, random thoughts, or, worst of all, good fortune:

♦   The objective of the report is more clearly defined.

♦   All the facts that will be needed are clearly identified.

♦   Unnecessary facts will not be included.

♦   The links between the key concepts and facts will immediately be recognisable because of the proximity and connection.

♦   The nature of the structure allows for easy addition of new thoughts and information.

The open-ended nature of a mind map will enable your brain to make new connections far more readily. Expect to be surprised.

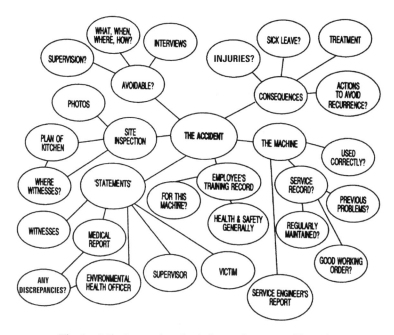

Fig. 1.   Mind mapping the information you will need.

At this stage what matters is that a **complete picture of information requirements** is seen to emerge. How far does the picture radiate naturally from the central objective? If a thought or fact or idea does not radiate, it will be difficult to make the report coherent and interesting. More importantly, it will not support your objective, so it has no place in the report.

PREPARING YOUR SKELETAL FRAMEWORK

You are now in a position to think about the overall **plan** of your report. This is known as the **skeletal framework**. It is like drawing up the plans for a new house. Not only will it show its overall **structure**, it will also remind you of the materials (**information**) you will need to gather before the process of construction can begin.

A number of significant benefits will accrue in constructing a skeletal framework. In particular, it will enable the writer:

♦ to be sure there is no misunderstanding over the Terms of Reference

♦ to have an overview of the entire report

♦ to be reminded of what information must be collected, what is already available and what is not needed

♦ to order his or her thoughts before considering how they should be expressed

♦ to appreciate the significance of, and the relationship between the various items of information that will be gathered

♦ to identify any gaps in coverage or logic, and

♦ to maintain a sense of perspective while gathering this information and, later, when writing the report.

A well-planned skeletal framework is the **key** to effective report writing. There are three stages involved in the preparation of a skeletal framework:

♦ Write a **working title**.

♦ Consider the **overall structure** of the report.

♦ Consider how information will be presented **within the main body**.

The first step then is to write a working title, which defines the subject matter of the document. The title must accurately describe what the text is all about. For the planning phase, use a *functional* title rather than a creative, attention-grabbing title. For example, use *Why ABC should build a factory in Anytown*, rather than *Anytown: A Town of Growth*.

A functional **working title** is helpful in continually reminding you of the document's objective. Save the more creative title for the final, published version of the report, possibly adding the working title as the subtitle.

The second step is to consider the **overall structure**. Reports come in a variety of shapes and sizes and are made up of a variety of sections, or **components**. If you can design a suitable framework everything else will then fall into place. Always remember this adage: tell them what you are going to say, then say it, then tell them what you said. This may sound trite; it isn't, because it gives you the opportunity to highlight the most important parts of your report. Also, people tend to remember what they read first and last far more than what they read in the middle of any document (this phenomenon is known as the **effect of primacy and recency**).

So give them a **beginning**, a **middle** and an **end**. It is your task to select the most appropriate components to build up each of these main sections.

What options are available to you? All reports have a number of commonly recognised components, including:

The beginning

♦ Title page

♦ Foreword

♦ Preface

♦ Acknowledgements

♦ Contents page

♦ Summary or Abstract

♦ Introduction

The middle

♦ Main body, including substructures

The end

♦ Conclusions

♦ Recommendations

♦ Appendixes

♦ References

♦ Bibliography or Resources

♦ Glossary

♦ Index.

Do not be concerned about the large number of components that may be used; no report ever uses all of them. However, it is as well to know something about each of these components for two reasons:

— You can then choose the ones best suited to your report, and

— You may be asked to include one or more of them.

Let us take a look at each of these components. We'll consider the beginning and end first before going on to the middle, the main body of the report.

Title page

Every report should have a title page. This tells the reader (and any potential reader) what the report is about. A good title page will include the following information:

- The title.

- The name and position of the person who authorised the report.

- The name of the author(s).

- His, her or their position within the organisation.

- The name of the organisation.

- The date the report was issued.

- A reference number.

- Copyright information, if necessary.

- Its degree of confidentiality.

- The distribution list.

Title

The **title** should be clear, concise and relevant; restate your terms of reference in your own words. Do not choose a title which is similar to any other report title. Providing a **subtitle** is a good way of keeping the title crisp while also providing more detail about its content. Make sure the title is more prominent than any headings that appear in the report.

Authorisation

Then say who **commissioned** the report (for example, 'Produced at the request of . . .').

Names and dates

The decision about whether to give your **first name and any qualifications** you may have attained should be dictated by house-style. However, as a general rule, people within your organisation will not need to be reminded of your qualifications whereas relevant qualifications will add authority to a report which is distributed externally. In the same way it is not necessary to say that you work for ABC Ltd, if the report is for internal circulation alone. The **date** on the report should be the date it was actually *issued*, which is not necessarily the date it was printed. Write this issue date in full to avoid possible ambiguities. For example, 12.8.12 means 12th August 2012, in Britain. In the USA it means 8th December 2012.

Reference number

The **reference number** given to the report will depend on company practice. Some organisations number all reports sequentially; others do so by department and yet others add some personal reference (perhaps the initials of the author).

Copyright

The decision whether to refer to **copyright** depends on the nature of the report. For the report writer the main interest in the English law of copyright is its intention to prevent the copying of a 'substantial part' of any literary work without permission. The word 'literary' covers any work expressed in printing or writing, provided it is substantial enough to have involved some literary skill and labour of composition. If you wish to know more about this, refer to the current edition of the *Writers' and Artists' Yearbook* at your local reference library.

Confidentiality

You may decide to stamp your report '**Secret**' or '**Confidential**'. The latter is a particularly useful marking when the report is about a member of staff, as it would be a strong defence against any subsequent charge of libel. Again you may wish to refer to the current edition of the *Writers' and Artists' Yearbook* for further information. However, do not overdo it. The most routine reports arouse exceptional interest when marked 'Secret'. Conversely a report giving a foolproof method of how to become a National Lottery Millionaire would probably go unnoticed as long as it was not given a security marking.

Distribution

Finally, the title page should include the **distribution list** of the report. Ask the person who requested the report to tell you who should see it. Their names will generally be listed in order of seniority. However, if you foresee any problems or disputes, perhaps because of internal politics, or if the report is to be sent outside your organisation, list the recipients alphabetically or by geographical location. Also remember to include at least one copy for file. Record this at the foot of the list.

Foreword

This component is rarely used in a report. When it is included it is generally not written by the report writer, but by an invited acknowledged expert in the field – perhaps the person who commissioned the report. A foreword should be concise.

Preface

This is another uncommon component. It is used when a writer wishes to convey some personal background details behind the report's production.

Acknowledgements

This section is used to convey your thanks to people and/or organisations who helped during the preparation of the report. For example they may have provided information, help, finance, or granted permission for you to use some copyright material. Do not go over the top with your thanks and try to keep them balanced and in perspective. For example, you may 'wish to record (your) thanks to Mr X' (who assisted you for an hour) and later 'to convey (your) special thanks to Mrs Y' (who helped for a week).

If a large number of people assisted you it may not be possible, or even desirable, to name them all. One way of getting round this is 'to thank the management and staff of ABC Ltd'. Alternatively, you could record a blanket acknowledgement such as: 'I also wish to thank everyone else who assisted during the preparation of this report'. In this way you are covered if you have forgotten to mention somebody by name.

As a general rule it is unnecessary to express your gratitude to people who would have been expected to help you (such as your staff), unless they made some special effort on your behalf. Read acknowledgements in books – including this one – to see how they should be written. Sometimes this section is placed towards the end of the report.

Contents page

A contents page is essential for any report exceeding three pages. It should be on a separate sheet of paper and it should list the various sections of the report in the order in which they appear. The headings on the contents page must be identical to those used in the text, with the appropriate page (and/or paragraph) number alongside them. If you have used more than just one or two illustrations then provide a separate list of these below the section headings. Your page numbering and paragraph numbering systems should be simple and consistent.

Summary or abstract or synopsis

This component is particularly useful when you have a diverse readership. It has two functions:

♦ To provide a precis of what the recipient is about to read or has just read.

♦ To provide an outline of the report if the recipient is not going to read the entire report.

An average manager's reading speed is between 200 and 250 words per minute, and he or she comprehends only 75 per cent of this. It is therefore extremely important to highlight the **salient facts** and the **main conclusions and recommendations**, if any. Obviously it cannot be written until *after* the other components of the report. Keep it concise;

it should never exceed one page. Do not introduce any matter which is not covered within the text of the report.

A summary *could* contain just five paragraphs:

◆ Intention (your purpose and scope)

◆ Outline (what was done and how it was done)

◆ Main findings

◆ Main conclusions

◆ Main recommendations (if necessary).

As a general rule, the more senior the reader, the less detail he or she will require. For this reason a reader is sometimes sent a summary *instead* of the entire report. When this is done the covering letter should offer a copy of the full report, if required.

Introduction

This section sets the scene. While the title page gives a broad indication of the subject, the introduction tells the reader what it is all about. A good introduction will engage the readers' interest and include everything that they will need to know before moving on to the main body of the report. It will contain certain essential preliminaries which would not be weighty enough individually to justify headings of their own. These might include:

◆ Why was the report written? Who requested it, and when?

◆ What were your terms of reference? *Always* refer to these in the introduction.

◆ What resources were available to you? (For example, staff, time and equipment.)

♦ What limitations, if any, did you work under? What were the reasons for this? (For example, 'The report does not analyse departmental expenditure in June because the figures were not available.')

♦ What sources of information did you use? How did you obtain this information?

♦ What were your methods of working? A technical report will require a technical explanation of methods used. (Some writers prefer to provide this information in an appendix.)

♦ How is the report structured? Why did you choose this method of presentation? This explanation helps your readers find their way around the report and shows the logic of the layout.

In some reports the first two of these preliminaries are called **aims** and the others are known collectively as **scope**.

Reports should not be anonymous documents, so it is usual for the name and signature of the author to appear immediately below the introduction. Some organisations prefer the signature to appear under the writer's name on the title page. Either way, it is best to sign every copy rather than simply sign and photocopy the master copy. In the case of professional firms preparing reports for clients, it is customary for only the name of the practice to be given. This indicates the joint responsibility of the partnership. The identity of the author is denoted by the reference.

Conclusions

Your conclusions should link your terms of reference (what you were trying to do, as stated in your introduction) with your findings (what you found out, as presented in your main body). They should flow naturally from your evidence and arguments; there must be no surprises. Conclusions should always be:

- ◆ clearly and simply stated

- ◆ objective and not exaggerated

- ◆ written with the likely impact on the reader clearly in mind.

Recommendations

Do not make any recommendations unless your terms of reference empower you to do so. While conclusions refer to the *past* and/or the *present*, recommendations look to the *future*. Any comment not concerned with the future has no place as a recommendation. Your recommendations should follow logically from your conclusions. Therefore, once again, there should be no surprises.

Effective recommendations are concise and to the point. They are also specific. For example, management may need to know what should be done by whom to overcome a specific problem; it will not want to be told that some undefined action should be taken by some unidentified individual for no apparent reason.

Your recommendations must also be realistic. Perhaps the security at a warehouse should be improved. If so, do not risk the rejection of a sensible recommendation, and the general undermining of the credibility of your report, by asking for too much. It is not really reasonable or feasible to expect it to be protected as thoroughly as Fort Knox.

So think carefully about the implications of all your recommendations; talk to the people involved and, where necessary, try to come to sensible compromises. Jaw is better than war.

A good way to check whether your recommendations are well-written is to extract them from the rest of the report and then read them in isolation. Do they still make sense? If not, re-draft them until they do.

Appendixes

The purpose of an appendix is to supplement the information contained in the main body of the report. It is a way of providing adequate detail for readers who require it without breaking the thread of the main body. But how do you know what information to put in appendixes, what to include in the main body and what to exclude from the report altogether? Figure 2 is an example of an algorithm that will help you decide the answer. Start at the top left.

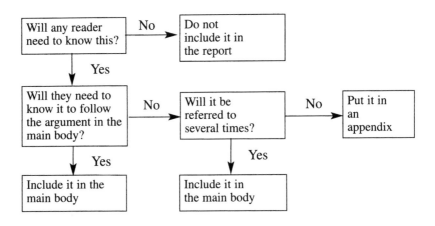

Fig. 2.   An algorithm.

Appendixes are useful as a way of:

♦ Meeting the needs of a diverse readership – some people will want/ need to refer to them while others will not. Appendix 1, on page 199, serves this purpose.

♦ Presenting documentary evidence to support arguments in the main body (for example, correspondence, instructions, forms, standard letters, questionnaires, maps, charts and so on). Appendix 2, on page 209, fulfils this function.

♦ Substantiating and/or amplifying findings in the main body.

♦ Providing detailed results of experiments or investigations.

♦ Presenting summaries of results obtained elsewhere.

♦ Presenting statistical or comparative information.

♦ Illustrating relationships or relative proportions by means of charts and diagrams.

♦ Explaining systems or procedures by flow charts and/or words.

An appendix is useless, however, unless it is clearly referred to in the main body of the report and in the contents list. *Tell* the readers why they may wish to refer to it.

References

This section provides full details of the books, journals, on-line sources and other materials which have been specifically mentioned in the text, or from which extracts have been quoted. There are a number of ways in which this can be done, but the most common methods are either to list them alphabetically, by author's surname, or in the order in which they are cited throughout the report.

Appendix 1 outlines the way to reference a report using the Harvard system, a method favoured by many educational institutions. However, as always, it is important that you establish precisely how *your* report should be referenced, and then to follow that method.

Bibliography or Resources

A bibliography also gives full details of every publication referred to in the text. However, unlike a reference section, it may also include books and journals *not* referred to. A bibliography is useful when you have a diverse readership since it can provide separate lists for **background reading**, **further reading** and **recommended reading**.

Strictly speaking, a bibliography is a list of *books*. However, nowadays other non-printed sources, such as on-line materials, are often also included. Some report writers prefer to re-name the section as **Resources**, thereby leaving no doubt in the reader's mind that *all* sources are included. Whichever heading you choose, details should be given in the same format as are references, and it is customary to list them alphabetically by the surname of the author or by the title of the book.

Glossary

A glossary is necessary when you have used a good deal of specialised or technical vocabulary. It is another useful device to help meet the needs of a diverse readership, some of whom will be familiar with the terminology and some of whom will not be. Make sure your definitions are authoritative, precise and up-to-date (words come and go and some change their meaning over time). For this reason it is important that your dictionary or reference book is a current edition.

List the words alphabetically and place the section towards the end of the report. However, if a large number of readers will need to familiarise themselves with the vocabulary before reading the report, it is better to place the glossary at the beginning.

Index

An index is necessary only for a large report. It should contain more entries than a contents page and it is perfectly acceptable for it to be presented in two or three columns. List items alphabetically and place the index at the end of the report.

Facilities for providing at least a basic index should be found in most word processors. However, always check any computer-generated index very carefully or the silliest mistakes can go undetected. In particular think about:

♦ the *meaning* of a word, and

♦ the *context* in which a word is used.

Some words are spelt the same way but have different meanings, such as bank (an establishment where money is deposited) and bank (the sloping ground on each side of a river). Make sure your index reflects the true *meaning* of a word. Some indexes do not. This excerpt is taken from page 19 of a report on local sports and recreational amenities:

> The Leader of the Council stated: 'The proposal to extend the sports centre will, of course, be considered'.

The relevant index entry read:

Course,
      golf-, 11
      of-, 19
      race-, 13

Equally importantly, watch out for the *context*. The following example comes from a law report:

> Mr Justice Straw said that he had a great mind to commit the man for trial.

In the index we find:

> Straw (Mr Justice), his great mind, 14

Main body

The final step is to consider how information should be presented **within the main body** of the report. If you have already mind mapped the information you will need to obtain (page 9), you can now re-shape this material into a structure that your readers will find both *acceptable* and *intelligible*.

The report on the accident in the canteen would be confusing if it simply recorded the supervisor's, doctor's and engineer's comments in turn. An improvement would be to extract the related parts of their respective evidence and to record them together within appropriate sections, or *categories* of the report.

Different levels of category must be organised into a *hierarchy*, with the title at the top of the hierarchy. **Level 1 categories** are based on *the broad areas that are to be covered*; **Level 2 categories** relate to the *more detailed findings* which *collectively* cover each of these broad areas:

Working title: Results of Investigation into the Canteen Accident at ABC Ltd.

Level 1 categories: The accident; The consequences; Condition of the machine; Employee training provided

Level 2 categories: What it was; Where it occurred; When it occurred; How it occurred (collectively covering 'The accident'); Injuries sustained; Treatment required; Absence from work resulting; Actions taken to avoid recurrence (collectively covering 'The consequences'); ... and so on.

In addition to the hierarchical organisation, each module, or group of categories must be put into a *logical order*. Categories can be considered as one of two types: *verbs* (relating to sequences, actions, events) and *nouns* (relating to people, places, ideas).

♦ **Verb categories** describe **actions**, something that **moves or changes over a period of time**; they involve **time-sequence information**, such as when each of several events occurred or how to perform the steps of a procedure. This book is structured in this way.

♦ **Noun categories** tell about something at **a specific point in time**; they include such descriptions as **who, what, why** and **where**.

Verb categories are usually arranged chronologically according to *order of occurrence*: sooner before later (e.g. procedure 1 before procedure 2, cause before effect, stimulus before response, problem before solution, question before answer):

Working title: Introducing Networks

♦ Using the network: overview

♦ Setting up your computer to use the network

♦ Sharing your folders or printers

♦ Using resources located on other computers

♦ Connecting to the Internet.

Noun categories are sequenced according to *quantity* (e.g. more before less), *quality* (e.g. better before worse), *space* (e.g. high before low), *alphabet* (e.g. A before B), or some other comparative or otherwise logical measure:

Working title: Comparison of Top Three Job Candidates
♦ Chris Brown
♦ Kim Jones
♦ Pat Smith

Once these three stages have been completed (working title; overall structure; order of information within the main body), the categories must be suitably numbered:

Results of Investigation into Canteen Accident at ABC Ltd.

1 Summary

2 Introduction

3 The accident

    3.1   What it was

    3.2   Where it occurred

    3.3   When it occurred

    3.4   How it occurred

4 The consequences

    4.1   Injuries sustained

    4.2   Treatment required

    4.3   Absence from work resulting

    4.4   Actions taken to avoid recurrence

5 Condition of the machine

    5.1   Condition at the time of the accident

    5.2   Previous service and maintenance record

6 Employee training provided

    6.1   General health and safety training

    6.2   Specific training relating to the operation of this machine

7 Conclusions

8 Recommendations

Appendixes

    1   Plan of kitchen

    2   Photographs of kitchen and machine

    3   Report of Environmental Health Officer

    4   Statement from accident victim

    5   Statement from supervisor

    6   Statement from Witness A

    7   Statement from doctor

    8   Statement from service engineer

    9   Service record of machine

    10   Training record of accident victim

TESTING AND REVISING YOUR SKELETAL FRAMEWORK

At this stage, conduct the first test on each component and the other tests on each module, or group of categories within the main body, starting with the Level 1 categories and then progressing module by module to the most detailed level of the hierarchy:

♦ **Necessity test:** Is each component necessary? For example: Is the Title Page necessary? The answer must be 'Yes' because it identifies the report to the reader. Or: Is the Glossary necessary? If all your readers know (or at least are likely to know) the meaning of all the technical words used, the answer will be 'No'. In that case remove it from the skeletal framework since it would serve no useful purpose.

♦ **Inclusion test:** Given the heading of the module, are all appropriate items included? If not, restrict the scope of the heading to fit the items that are present, or add the missing items.

♦ **Exclusion test:** Given the heading of the module, are all inappropriate items excluded? If not, delete the inappropriate items, or expand the heading to fit all the items in the module.

♦ **Hierarchy test:** Are the items in the module hierarchically parallel? Headings of similar rank should represent topics of roughly equal importance. If they are not, move the problem items to the appropriate level.

♦ **Sequence test:** Are the items in the appropriate sequence? Determine whether the module is of the verb or noun type, and then decide whether the sequence is most appropriate for each module.

♦ **Language test:** Are the items in the module grammatically parallel (e.g. all verb types ending in *-ing* or all nouns types ending with the word *Department*)? If not, change the wording to achieve consistency.

◆ **Numbering test:** Is the numbering system appropriate and consistent? Remember that the initial Level 1 category numbers will need to have been reserved for each component of the report that will appear *before* the main body (e.g. 1 Summary; 2 Introduction). Then you must ask yourself whether all Level 1 categories are numbered consistently (3, 4, 5). Similarly, are all Level 2 categories numbered rationally (3.1, 3.2, 4.1, 4.2, 4.3)?

These seven tests collectively provide a comprehensive yet relatively simple writing tool. Important benefits will accrue from consistently applying them:

◆ they ensure the structural soundness of the text

◆ they make the subsequent writing process much more straight-forward

◆ they ensure that text will be easier to read and understand.

SUMMARY

◆ It is essential to prepare and plan your report very carefully. This process will greatly reduce the time and effort subsequently on writing and re-writing the report by:

—reminding you of the message you need to convey in order to get the results you want

—providing you with a logical and considered structure which will help you identify any gaps or illogicalities

—enabling you to obtain an overview of the entire report, thereby helping you to maintain a sense of perspective

—providing you with clear guidelines as you collect and handle the information, and then write the report.

- Be crystal clear about your objective. Why are you writing this report? What effect do you want it to have on your readers? The status quo is not an option, or there would be no need for the report to be written.

- Find out as much about your audience as possible. You will say different things, and in different ways, to help achieve your objective when addressing different people.

- Think carefully about the information you will need. Talk to the person who asked you to write the report and speak to any key readers. What would they like to see included? Don't include anything unless it is relevant and it helps you achieve your objective. Good report writing is often more about what to leave out than what to put in.

- Spend as much time as is necessary in designing, testing and revising your skeletal framework. It is the **key** to effective report writing. It should not only cover the **structure** and **content** of the report, but also the **relative significance** and **relationship between the main findings**. It has been estimated that 75 per cent of the time spent on effective report writing is devoted to planning, and 75 per cent of that 75 per cent is spent on preparing the optimal framework for *any particular* report.

2
Collecting and Handling Information

Once you have carefully planned your report, it is time to carry out all the work that will be necessary before you can actually write it. In other words, you are now ready to undertake your project or investigation. Your task is to collect and handle enough relevant information to enable you to put flesh on the bones of your skeletal framework. These are the stages your research should follow:

♦ Locate sources of relevant information.

♦ Obtain the information.

♦ Sort and group your findings.

♦ Evaluate your findings.

♦ Prioritise your findings.

♦ Check your findings.

♦ Acknowledge your sources.

It is quite possible to write a poor report even after doing good research, but it is impossible to write a good report after doing poor research. The moral is clear: good research is *essential*.

LOCATING SOURCES OF RELEVANT INFORMATION

By now you will have identified the information you require, bearing in mind:

- the precise purpose of the report

- the needs of your readers

- your objective(s)

- your resources

- your skeletal framework.

There are four sources of information available to you:

- People

- Books and other publications

- Information available electronically

- Events and places.

The information you will need may be found under any or all of these categories, so you might consider each in turn.

People

You may be able to obtain the information you require from the local, national, or even the international community. Here are some possibilities:

- your colleagues

- members of the public

- politicians

- producers

- manufacturers

- retailers

- federations

♦ unions

♦ pressure groups

♦ international organisations.

It is impossible to give details of the vast number of potential sources available to you. However, here is one service that every report writer should be aware of:

The Information Bureau
Formerly the Telegraph Information Service, the Information Bureau has a reputation for being able to answer almost any question, either instantly over the telephone or, after a telephoned request, by fax the same day. A fee is charged for each enquiry.

The Information Bureau
51 Battersea Business Centre
103 Lavender Hill
London SW11 5QL
Tel: (020) 7924 4414
Fax: (020) 7738 2513
Email: info@informationbureau.co.uk

Books and other publications
Perhaps the information can be extracted from a printed source, such as:

♦ encyclopaedias

♦ reference books

♦ text books

♦ guides

♦ handbooks

- journals and magazines

- newspapers

- maps and charts

- previous reports

- correspondence

- minutes.

Information available electronically

The information that a computer can put at your fingertips is almost limitless. You can often have free on-line access to a veritable cornucopia of information, providing you are prepared to put some time and effort into tracking down the facts and figures you really want. The sources you are most likely to encounter are:

- websites (including social network sites)

- electronic books and journals

- on-line databases

- JISCmail/Listserv email lists

- Usenet newsgroups/Bulletin boards/Blogs

- personal emails

- audio visual materials.

The information superhighway

The Internet was once the exclusive province of US government-sponsored research scientists and academics, but now it provides entry to a vast array of information from computer systems around the world to almost anybody. Today advances in information technology provide unprecedented opportunities for report writers to communicate directly with experts around the globe.

Events and places

Perhaps the information you require is available at one or more events or places. Here is a small sample of some local, national and international possibilities:

♦ libraries

♦ learning resources centres

♦ research institutions

♦ exhibitions

♦ museums

♦ galleries

♦ laboratories

♦ theatres

♦ concerts

♦ talks.

Libraries
In addition to local, university and college libraries, many government departments and business organisations run libraries that are open to the public. These include:

♦ The City Business Library (London): (020) 7332 1812 (Main switchboard).
pro@cityoflondon.gov.uk

♦ Westminster Reference Library (London): (020) 7641 1300.
referencelibrarywc2@westminster.gov.uk

♦ The Central Statistical Office (Newport, South Wales): (01633) 456 582.
library.enquiries@ons.gov.uk

The British Library is a copyright library. That is, it is entitled to receive a copy of every book published in the UK. The library is divided into sections by subject and the following list gives the telephone numbers of some of its departments:

♦ Main Switchboard: (0870) 444 1500.

♦ Visitor Information: (01937) 546 060.

♦ Business Information: (020) 7412 7454.

♦ Newspaper Library: (020) 7412 7353.

♦ Patents: (020) 7412 7454.

♦ Science, Technology and Medicine: (020) 7412 7288.

It is best to phone or email before you visit any unfamiliar library to check opening times and confirm that you will be allowed in.

OBTAINING THE INFORMATION

Information can be gathered by one or more of these methods:

♦ experimentation

♦ reading

♦ listening

♦ observation

♦ interview

♦ letter

♦ telephone call

♦ questionnaire

♦ research on the Internet.

When you come to draft and then finalise your report, you will need to acknowledge all the sources of the information you have used. For this reason it is a good idea to maintain an on-going record as you collect your material. This can be done either on index cards or on a computer-based equivalent.

We will return to this aspect of effective report writing on page 55 and again at Appendix 1. However, it is important to appreciate the need for keeping such records *during* the research stage of your project, not *after* it, when it may be too late. Of course, you may ultimately decide not to use one or more of your items of research. However, it is prudent to keep record of *all* your potential sources as you gather them.

You must have enough details to enable you to accurately and comprehensively acknowledge all the people, books and other publications, information obtained electronically, and any events and places you have visited, that you mention in your report without needing to re-perform any research task, or contact anybody for a second or subsequent time, or rely upon your memory, or – and worst or all – trust in guesswork.

Experimentation

An experiment should be carried out by a trained scientist who will design and perform it in an acceptable way. The experiment should be written up as follows:

♦ Begin with a dated heading stating clearly the **objective of the experiment**: 'To study . . .', 'To find . . .'.

♦ Give a brief account of the **theory** underlying the experiment.

♦ Provide a **hypothesis** (suggested answer), if you have one.

- Give a clear and full account of **how the experiment was carried out**. It is usually necessary to provide a **diagram** of the apparatus used.

- Provide a complete list of the **readings** you obtained.

- Provide a full **statement of the final result**, showing the estimated limits of error.

- **Conclude** with a clear and concise statement of what your results lead you to infer or deduce about the problem posed. If you have a hypothesis, refer to it here. If you have any relevant views on the experiment or the result obtained, include these. Also, if you believe that the experiment could have been improved in some way, explain why and how.

Reading

The way you read should vary according to the **complexity** of the material and the **reasons** for reading it. If you are reading to understand, absorb or master a topic you must read it slowly. If you are reading a novel for entertainment you can read it quickly.

Try the SQ3R method of reading:

S   Survey
Q   Question
R   Read
R   Recall
R   Review.

Survey

This is the preliminary review of the book or article. It involves skimming (glancing over the material and getting the feel of it) and scanning (looking at specific aspects of the publication – the title, the author, the date, the preface, the introduction, the contents, any chapter summaries and the index). In the case of a book, it is also a good idea to read the first and last paragraphs of potentially relevant chapters and the first and last sentences of a sample of paragraphs within these chapters. This scanning should give you an overall impression of the publication, such as:

♦ Is it pitched at the right level?

♦ Is it up to date?

♦ Is the author a recognised authority in the field?

♦ Is the book factual or based on opinion?

Question
Then ask yourself these questions:

♦ What would I expect to gain if I read some or all of this material?

♦ Is some or all of the material directly relevant to my report?

♦ Does some or all of it provide a useful background to my report?

Read
Once you have decided to read some or all of a publication, divide your reading into manageable segments, probably chapters or sections. Read any summaries or conclusions *first*. Next, read the chapter or section quickly to get a grasp of the material. Finally, read it again, more slowly, and ensure you understand it.

Recall
Think about the main ideas and facts you have been reading about and make notes of them.

Review

Are you satisfied that you have gained what you expected through your reading? Have you gathered the information you will need to help put the flesh on your skeletal framework?

Listening

Some researchers suggest that we function at only 25 per cent efficiency and rarely remember what we have heard. In one investigation the proportion of information which was correctly transmitted from a senior director through middle and line management to operative staff was as low as 20 per cent. Such ineffective listening can be responsible for the following:

♦ Accidents at work.

♦ Production breakdowns.

♦ Lost sales and customers.

♦ Poor morale.

♦ Personality clashes.

♦ Inaccurate communication.

So how can you improve your listening skills?

Do not:

♦ Assume that the topic is boring or irrelevant. A good listener sifts, screens and hunts for relevant information.

♦ Criticise delivery or presentation; concentrate on the content.

♦ Submit to emotional phrases. Do not allow the use of phrases which you loathe to reduce your listening capacity.

♦ Become overstimulated. Do not try to think of 'clever' or embarrassing questions. Use your time positively, listening and structuring your thoughts.

♦ Listen only to facts. Think also of the main ideas, concepts, structure and how the values, attitudes and prejudices of the speaker affect the presentation.

♦ Expect the speaker to structure the talk to suit your needs. As you take notes, follow the speaker's approach, otherwise your structure will not fit in with the concepts and ideas presented. You can rearrange your notes later.

♦ Remain passive. Listening is an active process, so stay alert.

♦ Tolerate distractions. If you cannot hear the speaker, or if you are too hot or too cold, then say so.

♦ Listen to only what you want to hear. Be willing to consider arguments and evidence which oppose your views. Be aware of your prejudices.

♦ Evade difficult subjects. Face problems head on.

♦ Waste your thinking potential. People normally talk at about 125 words per minute, but they listen and can think at about 400 words per minute. The differential of 275 words per minute is a breeding ground for day dreaming.

Do:

♦ Run ahead of the speaker. What has been said? What might be said? What is this all leading to? What are the implications of this message? By asking yourself these questions you will improve your concentration.

♦ Examine the evidence presented. Is it accurate, objective and complete? Is it strong or weak?

- Recap every few minutes in order to avoid day dreaming.

- Remember that listening is an active process and is therefore very hard work.

You have two ears and one mouth. Try to use them in roughly that proportion.

Observation

Sometimes the best way to find out is simply to observe. For example, you may be trying to find out how much traffic passes Anytown Primary School. According to your purpose you might need to break this figure down to the types of vehicle, specific days, and possibly to different times of year. The simplest way of recording your results is to use a series of tally sheets like the one illustrated in Figure 3.

Interview

Interviewing is a skilled technique and few people do it well. While the interview should appear to be reasonably casual, it must be planned and structured. Follow these key steps:

Step 1 Greet the interviewee in a friendly manner. Avoid too much small talk and maintain a professional image.

Step 2 Explain the precise purpose of the interview. What do you want to find out? Let the interviewee know that his or her input will be valued.

Step 3 Ask your questions. Use open questions (who, what, when, why, where, how), and try to avoid yes/no answers. Listen and show you understand. Then follow up with secondary questions. Give the interviewee time to answer. Cover one topic at a time; try not to 'hop about'. Empathise – do not judge or be seen to take sides.

Traffic Passing Anytown Primary School (west – east)

Tally sheet no.:
Date:
Time:
Name of observer:

	No.	%
Cars		
Buses		
Lorries		
Vans		
Motor Bikes		
Other (specify)		
Total		

Fig. 3.   A tally sheet.

Step 4 Sum up the interview to check your understanding of facts, opinions and circumstances.

Step 5 Thank the interviewee for his or her co-operation.

Letter

If you decide to ask for information by letter, remember to:

♦ Name the person you are writing to and give his or her designation and organisation (for example, Miss V. Rich, Chief Finance Officer, Midshire County Council).

♦ Give the letter a heading.

♦ Explain the purpose of your report in the first paragraph.

♦ Courteously ask for the information you require. Keep it concise but comprehensive.

♦ If possible, draw a table where this information can be inserted.

♦ Send the letter as early as possible and tactfully request a reply within two or three weeks.

♦ Enclose a stamped addressed envelope.

♦ Conclude the letter by thanking the person in anticipation.

Telephone call

Sometimes you can obtain the information you need by making one or more telephone calls. However, this method is not recommended when the information is likely to be fairly complex and/or there are figures involved (for example, 'Did she say £4, £14, or £40?'). Telephone calls are most appropriate when you know the person and when your questions are straightforward (often requiring no more than yes/no answers).

If you do decide to telephone, write down the questions you want to ask and have a pen and a few sheets of paper handy. If you are using a mobile, ensure you have adequate battery life and talktime. Then follow these key steps:

Step 1 Give your name ('Good morning, I'm . . .').

Step 2 Ask for the right person ('May I speak to . . . ?').

Step 3 Explain why you are telephoning. Emphasise that you are not selling anything! ('I'm phoning about a report I am preparing on . . .').

Step 4 Politely ask for the information you require. Let them know that their input will be appreciated ('I would be extremely grateful if you could help me on one or two points . . .').

Step 5 Thank the person by name.

Speak distinctly, deliberately and a little more slowly than you normally do. Make your voice pleasant, cheerful and positive. Keep the conversation short without ever being abrupt.

Questionnaire

This method of information gathering involves questioning a sample of people (respondents). Questionnaires seek two kinds of information:

♦ Factual. For example, 'How often do you *buy* Product A?'

♦ Opinion. For example, 'What do you *think* of Product A?'

Such a survey is necessary only if the information sought is not already available, or if the information is out of date. There are two important points to bear in mind when producing a questionnaire. First, you will need to approach members of the public and they have no obligation to assist you, so ensure that your questions (and your general approach) are courteous. Second, make sure that your questions are relevant to the subject of your report. Figure 4 is an example of a simple questionnaire to find out what schoolchildren think about their school meals.

Here is a checklist for a good questionnaire:

♦ Does it have a title?

♦ Does it have a reference or questionnaire number?

♦ Does it record the name of the interviewer?

- Is it well spaced?

- Does it explain the purpose of the questionnaire?

- Where appropriate, does it emphasise that all replies will be treated confidentially?

- Is it clear and unambiguous?

- Is it simple?

- Is it logically developed?

- Does it ask one question at a time (not two or more questions at the same time)?

- Does it require definite answers?

- Does it avoid leading questions? (Ask: 'What do you think of product A?' *not*: 'Product A is fantastic. Do you agree?'.)

- Does it avoid an appeal for vanity? (Ask: 'Do you take regular exercise?', *not*: 'Most fit people exercise regularly. Do you?'.)

- Does it avoid an appeal to sympathy? (Ask: 'Should the Health Service be better funded?', *not*: 'People are dying needlessly. Should the National Health Service be better funded?'.)

- Where appropriate, does it leave sensitive areas until last (for example, the age of middle-aged or elderly respondents)?

- Is the questionnaire written in such a way that will make it straightforward to record and analyse your overall results?

- Has the questionnaire been 'pilot tested' among a small number of respondents to highlight any obvious errors, omissions, ambiguities and other shortcomings before the survey goes live?

School Meals Questionnaire

Questionnaire No.   Interviewer:

                                               Date:

'I am carrying out a survey on school meals on behalf of Midshire County Council. I wonder whether you would be willing to answer a few questions?

Ask the respondent

Q 1 Which class are you in?   Year 6   ☐
                                               Year 7   ☐
                                               Year 8   ☐
                                               Year 9   ☐
                                               Year 10   ☐
                                               Year 11   ☐

Q 2 Enter the sex of the respondent   Male   ☐
                                               Female   ☐

Q 3 How often do you have school meals?   Every day   ☐
                                               most days   ☐
                                               2 or 3 days per week ☐
                                               Not often   ☐
                                               Never   ☐

If the answer is 'Every day', go straight to Q 5

Q 4 When you don't have a school dinner,
     what do you do instead?   Go home to dinner   ☐
                                               Buy dinner elsewhere   ☐
                                               Bring own food   ☐
                                               Have no dinner   ☐
                                               Other (specify)   ☐

Q 5 Do you think that school meals are: Very good?   ☐
                                               Quite good?   ☐
                                               Average?   ☐
                                               Bad?   ☐
                                               Awful?   ☐

Thank respondent for helping

Fig. 4.   A questionnaire.

Once you have designed your questionnaire and amended it as necessary, you must decide on sampling methods. No strict rules can be laid down for sampling. The methods used will depend on the circumstances of the case, but unless the methods are **random** the reliability of the results is no more than a matter of opinion.

The following are three common sampling techniques:

Simple random sampling
This is a quick and simple method, by which every person or item has an equal chance of being selected. If you want to select 10 per cent of a population of 100, simply take 10 names out of a hat containing the 100 names.

Systematic random sampling
Again, every person or item has an equal chance of being selected, but the choice is made to a prearranged plan (though it is still random). For example, select every 100th name on the electoral register.

Quota sampling
This is used to get a balanced view from people in the street based on age, sex and possibly social class. For example, select twenty males, aged 16–20; twenty males, 21–25; twenty males, 26–30; twenty females, 16–20; twenty females, 21–25; twenty females, 26–30.

Finally, you should be aware of **errors that can occur** owing to **bias** in sampling or questioning. Here are some ways of avoiding bias:

In sampling:

♦ Do not **deliberately** select people or items. All selections must be **random**.

♦ Do not substitute or replace items selected randomly. For example, if you decide to question somebody from every twentieth house, do not change to the twenty-first if you do not receive a reply at the twentieth. The householders may be at work and should not be excluded for this reason. Call at a different time or on a different day.

♦ Do not deliberately omit items that should be selected randomly. If you need to select ten males, aged 16–20, approach a random selection – not, for instance, just young professionals.

In questioning:

♦ Do not vary the wording of your questions.

♦ Do not ask leading questions.

♦ Do not ask questions which appeal to vanity.

♦ Do not ask questions which appeal to sympathy.

Research on the Internet

The Internet has made it possible to find vast amounts of information on just about every conceivable subject. To use the Internet efficiently, however, you need to keep a clear idea of the exact information you are seeking. It is all too easy to get side-tracked:

♦ **The Internet can take up all your research time**. Researching electronically can become a mesmerising activity, and you might find that after a pleasant afternoon you have found nothing of any value for your report.

♦ **Remember what you are trying to achieve**. Skip material that is only loosely related to your specific requirements.

♦ **Beware of the need to evaluate information obtained on the Internet**. Although there are many well-maintained and reliable websites, the quality and accuracy of statements on the Internet vary widely. Anyone can put up a website and can claim to be an authority. Content is frequently opinion-based or factually out-of-date.

Before you begin your research:

♦ Write down the questions you hope to answer.

♦ Spend time thinking about who would be likely to know the answers. The most efficient research method on the Internet is often simply to email the appropriate person or organisation.

♦ Develop a list of subtopics and synonyms that you can use as search terms.

Using a subject directory

One way to get plenty of information on your topic is to use a subject directory on the Web. One of the best known directories is *Yahoo!* (*http://dir.yahoo.com*), which contains tens of thousands of sites. Although it organises everything by categories, you can also search by keywords. Once you find your topic, *Yahoo!* gives you a list of relevant Web addresses (URLs) and a short description of the sites.

Using metasearchers

If the subject directory does not yield enough relevant information, there are plenty of **search engines** which seek to catalogue the ever-growing content on the Web. Use a **metasearcher**, such as *Dogpile* (*http://www.dogpile.com*), or *Google* (*http://www.google.com*). These will utilise a number of search engines simultaneously and organise the results. *Ask Jeeves* (*http://www.ask.co.uk*) will actually search for you based upon the question you pose. The same query will bring up different results with different search engines, so from the metasearcher's results you may find that one search engine is best for your topic. Metasearchers also save you time because they modify your phrases according to the rules of each specific search engine.

Using various combinations of search terms

Type the words you want the search engine to hunt for in the box provided on the screen. Every search program uses slightly different rules of operation, but most use two searching conventions:

◆ Quotation marks indicate that the phrase is to be treated as one search term – for example, "Westminster Abbey".

◆ 'Boolean operators' such as *and*, *or* and *not* tell the computer how to interpret your list of search terms. In general:

and specifies that both terms should appear.

or specifies that either term should appear.

not specifies that a term should not appear.

The trouble is search engines tend to provide you with either far too many references or far too few. If, in reality, there are 20 or 30 sites that would be of value to access, the search engine is likely to come up either with 2,000 or 3,000, or with 2 or 3!

If there is no match for your request:

◆ You may have misspelt one or more words.

◆ You may have used the wrong symbols or phrasing for that particular search engine.

◆ You may need to try a different search engine.

◆ You may have submitted too narrow a search. Try widening it from, say, *Edgbaston* to *Birmingham*. Once you find some sites, their links will take you to others.

- Give both the abbreviation and the full name, linked by *or* (*UN* or "*United Nations*")

- Try adding more alternatives – both more general and more specific:

  cereals, grain, wheat, maize, corn, rice, millet, sorghum, cornflakes, muesli, oatmeal, porridge.

- The information may be there, but your computer cannot reach it right now. Try again later.

If there are too many listings:

- Take a look at the first ten results to see if they coincide with your topic. For example, if an inquiry on uncultivated grain using the phrase "*wild oats*" yielded thousands of articles, and the first ten are all about indiscretions of youth, you'll need to rephrase the search.

- If the first ten listings are on your topic, skim a few of them to extract more search terms.

- Add more words to your search string, putting a more specific word first.

After a while, though, you will become more proficient in selecting the right syntax and combination of keywords that will bring you a manageable list and it will become almost second nature to find the most efficient routes as you *surf the net*, jumping from page to page and from site to site.

SORTING AND GROUPING YOUR FINDINGS

If the report has been well-planned, this process will be quite straightforward. Use the headings and sub-headings of your skeletal framework and make sure you have gathered enough relevant information to complete each section and subsection. If you need more information, gather it now – not once you have started to draft your report.

EVALUATING YOUR FINDINGS

There are two aspects to this evaluation:

♦   How *reliable* are the findings?

♦   How *significant* are the findings?

Consider each in turn.

How reliable are the findings?

There are four factors by which the reliability of information should be judged:

♦   accuracy

♦   objectivity

♦   completeness

♦   strength.

Accuracy

Sometimes you can check the data supplied. For example, are the **mathematical calculations** accurate? If there are too many to check, remember Pareto's principle which states that 80 per cent of what is important is represented by 20 per cent of what exists. Concentrate on this 20 per cent.

Information may also be inaccurate if it is out of date. In **experimental work**, was current equipment used? In **legal matters**, has account been taken of any recent and relevant legislation or case law? When **text books** have been consulted, were they the most recent editions?

Objectivity

When people have strongly held beliefs they will often see or hear things which support these beliefs, but they will not see or hear things which oppose them. For example, self-deception may cause results to be interpreted incorrectly. Going further, it is not unknown for people to perpetrate fraud, either to hoax or to provide 'evidence' to support preconceived ideas.

So ask yourself whether all the **major or relevant points of view** have been fairly represented. If the subject is controversial, the arguments for both (or all) cases should have been presented. At the very least, the person who provided the information should have made it clear that the views expressed are his or her own, and should then provide references to opposing viewpoints.

Finally, be very wary of statements without supporting evidence.

Completeness

In computer science a 'hash total' is used to ensure the completeness of a batch of records. However, it is often extremely difficult to prove that information is complete or, more accurately, that it is not incomplete. For example, we know of many animals that once inhabited the world. But how can we prove that they were the only ones? How can we prove that unicorns never existed? What you must ask yourself, therefore, is whether **all relevant information** has been provided and whether any attempt has been made to deceive or mislead by omission. Then look at it from the other side: is all the information provided relevant or is someone trying to 'blind you with science'?

Strength

Evidence is strong when:

♦ It can be verified or re-performed (for example, a scientific experiment).

- Independent observers have all come to the same conclusion(s).

- There have been a large number of consistent observations.

- It is in agreement with the general body of knowledge.

Conversely, evidence is weak when some or all of these conditions cannot be satisfied. Always differentiate between fact and opinion, and remember that the former provides the far stronger evidence.

How significant are the findings?

You must now step back and assess the implications of your findings. How material are they? Many report writers simply list every piece of information they have gathered without any consideration of its relative importance. This is a mistake because it implies that each is of equal weight. It is important to recognise that there will be a variety of interconnected causes for, and consequences of, an event – and these will *not* be of equal importance.

PRIORITISING YOUR FINDINGS

What you must do is highlight your most significant findings, and be prepared to explain carefully why they are so important. You may find it useful to amend your skeletal framework so that these key findings will not get lost somewhere within the main body of the report or in an appendix. But don't overdo it: the more things you highlight in the main body and summary, the less powerful each so-called 'highlight' will become.

At the other extreme, ask yourself whether everything you have found is worth recording in the report. Perhaps some findings should merely be placed in an appendix as evidence of work undertaken – or perhaps they should be omitted entirely. If your readers dismiss any of your findings as petty or irrelevant, this can undermine the entire report and severely damage your credibility.

As you prioritise your findings, continually remind yourself that your aim will be to tell your readers everything they need to know, but not to waste their time with trivia.

CHECKING YOUR FINDINGS

Before you conclude your investigation or project, you must be sure that:

♦ You have collected and handled all the information you will need to write the report.

♦ You are satisfied that all this information is accurate and reliable.

It is far better to fill in any gaps in your research now – or perhaps re-perform an experiment, or refer to some further management statistics, or confirm your understanding of the way a system operates – while you are still on site. Otherwise you may later have to rely on your memory, or on someone's uncorroborated evidence over the phone, or – and worst of all – trust to luck, before you can complete your draft report.

So ask yourself: Could I confidently write the report now, relying only on the information I have collected and handled? The investigation should not be wound up until the answer to this question is an unqualified 'Yes'.

ACKNOWLEDGING YOUR SOURCES

When you come to write your report you will need to clearly and accurately indicate each time you include ideas, theories, quotations or information provided by others to support your own work. Anything you use which was originally produced by someone else must be acknowledged, if it was drawn upon:

- as a general inspiration

- as a source of a particular theory, argument or viewpoint

- for specific information, such as statistics, examples or case studies

- for direct quotations (reproducing an author's precise words)

- for paraphrased texts and electronic information (where you have taken someone else's words but have changed them into your own).

There are a number of reasons why you need to do this:

- It is a courtesy to the person or persons whose ideas, findings or words you have drawn upon or referred to.

- It makes it clear to the reader that you are not trying to pretend someone else's work is your own, that is to say that you are not *plagiarising*.

- It helps your readers find the original texts, websites and the like, should they wish to.

- It helps *you* find these sources again, at any time in the future, should you need to.

- It adds authority to your work. People will have far more confidence in your assertions if they know where your information comes from, especially if it is provided by a recognised expert.

- It provides documentary evidence of the thoroughness and relevance of your research.

There are two places where you will need to acknowledge that you have included the work of others:

- In the Main Body or Appendixes, where you indicate the exact point at which you have referred to the work of someone else. This is known as *citing* or *in-text referencing*.

♦ At the end of your report in the References section, where you list all the sources you have used, or in the Bibliography or Resources section, where you include all these sources – *and* possibly also other potentially useful sources *not* referred to in the report. This is known as *referencing*.

There are a number of different conventions for citing and referencing a report. The important thing is to ensure you follow the method preferred by your organisation, or by the person who commissioned your report. Many academic institutions follow the Harvard system and this method is described in Appendix 1. Alternatively you may be expected to produce a **Bibliography**, a **Resources** section (see page 21), or perhaps to use **footnotes**. These list the reference at the foot of the relevant page, the end of the relevant section or towards the end of the report.

If you are uncertain whether a particular item requires a formal acknowledgement, always err on the side of caution: it is far better to acknowledge too much than too little.

SUMMARY

While it is quite possible to write a bad report after completing a good investigation or project, it is *impossible* to write a good report until you have successfully **located, obtained, sorted and grouped, evaluated, prioritised, checked** and **acknowledged** the right amount of relevant information.

Locating information

There are four sources of information available to you:

♦ people

♦ books and other publications

- information available electronically

- events and places.

Obtaining information

Information can be gathered from these sources by various methods, such as experimentation, interview and research on the Internet. Keep an on-going record of your sources.

Sorting and grouping information

Do this under the headings and sub-headings of the skeletal framework. Make sure you have gathered enough relevant information to be able to complete each section and sub-section of the report.

Evaluating information

Critically evaluate the evidence and arguments. Are they:

- Accurate?

- Objective?

- Complete?

- Strong?

How *significant* are your findings? Some will be far more important than others. As you review each finding ask yourself: So what?

Prioritising information

Highlight your most significant findings – but *only* your most significant findings. If necessary amend the skeletal framework to make your key findings prominent within the main body as well as in the summary. Use the rest of the main body and any appendixes to tell your readers everything they need to know, but do not bore them with trivia.

Checking information

Before the project is completed, make one final check to ensure you have gathered enough accurate, reliable and relevant information to enable you to write the entire report.

Acknowledging your sources

Remember that you will need to acknowledge all of your sources, both in the main body of the report (and in any appendices) and also in a Reference section, a Bibliography or a Resources section. So retain full details of all the information you collect and handle.

3
Writing and Revising Your Report

If sufficient time and thought have been devoted to preparing and planning, and possibly revising, the skeletal framework, and to collecting and handling the information, you will now have a practical blueprint for the entire report. Writing will entail amplifying the points in each section and 'putting flesh on the bones'.

The highly subjective and mentally demanding process of effective written communication is the subject of Chapter 4. This chapter is concerned with the *clinical* process of ordering, classifying and sequencing. The order of writing and reviewing is important, and should be as follows:

♦ Pre-write.

♦ Draft the main body and appendices.

♦ Review the main body and appendices.

♦ Draft the references, conclusions, recommendations, introduction and summary.

♦ Check and amend the report.

♦ Issue the report.

Consider each stage in turn.

PRE-WRITING

Take an overview of your report before you begin to draft it. There are five aspects to this (three if you are not making recommendations), namely:

- **Targeting**. Remember your readers. It is all too easy to write for yourself and not for them.

- **Outlining**. Bear in mind your purpose and objective(s). Make sure your outline (general plan) is just wide enough to encompass them – no more and no less.

- **Structuring**. Refer to your skeletal framework. Is it still the most suitable, or will it need to be revised, perhaps to highlight some particularly important finding?

- **Developing**. What will you recommend to overcome problems identified?

- **Checking**. Are you sure that these recommendations are practicable?

DRAFTING THE MAIN BODY AND APPENDIXES

These components should be written first. Begin with the section or subsection of the main body, or with the appendix you feel most confident about. There are two important reasons for doing this:

- For any writer there is little worse than the horror of facing that first blank page. By choosing to write what you find the easiest or most inviting, you avoid this initial trepidation by immediately getting down to writing.

- The more difficult parts of a project seem less daunting once the easier ones have been accomplished.

In the back of your mind you will be aware that this draft is likely to be amended. This is not a reason to treat it lightly. The better your first draft, the better your final draft will be. So write as if *this* is your final draft.

REVIEWING THE MAIN BODY AND APPENDIXES

Once you have written your detailed findings, try to forget about them for a while. Then come back with a fresh mind. Assess what you have *actually written* and how it *comes across*, rather than still thinking about what you had intended to write and get across. Put yourself in your readers' shoes and be highly self-critical. As you read and re-read your draft, you should:

- Assess whether the substructure of the main body (logical, sectional or creative) is really the most suitable one to present your facts and arguments.

- Examine the layout and general appearance.

- Determine whether the tone and balance are correct.

- Review the use and format of tabulations and appendixes.

- Check the accuracy of figures and calculations.

- Ensure you have acknowledged (cited) all of your sources.

- Check the use of English, punctuation and spelling.

This self-assessment should give you a good idea of whether it is necessary to re-structure your framework and/or re-write any of the main body or appendixes, in order to get your message across as you had intended.

DRAFTING THE REFERENCES, CONCLUSIONS, RECOMMENDATIONS, INTRODUCTION AND SUMMARY

These sections should not be written until *after* the main body and appendixes have been completed, reviewed and, where necessary, redrafted. Each of these sections can now be directly related to what has *actually* been written in the main body and appendixes. The first section can now be an accurate summary of the report. Another advantage of this approach is that it avoids the danger of writing the report twice: it is very easy for an introduction to develop into a report if the detailed findings have not been written first of all.

Most writers draft these sections in the order in which they appear above, namely:

♦ references

♦ conclusions

♦ recommendations

♦ introduction

♦ summary.

References

Once you have reviewed the main body and any appendices – and possibly re-structured your framework and/or re-written some parts of your text – you will need to formally acknowledge all your sources of information in a References section, a Bibliography or a Resources section. Whichever of these components you use, it should begin on a separate page from whatever immediately precedes it.

Conclusions, recommendations and introduction

Your conclusions must follow logically from your detailed findings. Your recommendations must follow logically from your conclusions.

Your introduction should include everything your readers need to know before they read the rest of the report.

Summary

While these sections are all important, you must pay particular attention to your summary. Make sure that the overall opinion is expressed accurately and unambiguously, and reflects the findings and comments given in the main body and appendices. It must be a true summary of the report and should highlight any areas requiring a particular emphasis. As already stated, the summary should stimulate the readers' interest by outlining:

◆ The salient facts.

◆ The main conclusions and recommendations.

Remember that it is intended to serve two overall functions:

◆ To provide a précis of what the recipient is going to read, or has just read.

◆ To provide an outline of the report if the recipient is not going to read any more of the report.

A summary must be interesting; if a reader finds it boring, the report will have failed.

CHECKING AND AMENDING THE REPORT

Hold it two weeks is a classic rule in advertising. For the report writer this may not be practicable. However, once you have completed your first draft, try to forget all about it for a few days – or at least a few hours. Then re-read it. Does it flow? Are there adequate links and signposts for the reader? Can you justify everything that you have written? Finally, ask yourself whether you would be willing to *say* what you have *written* to the recipients, face-to-face. If you would not be willing to say it, do not write it either.

Now print a copy of the document you have prepared on your word processor. It is usual for three people to be involved in checking and amending this first draft:

- yourself

- a colleague

- your line manager.

Your check

Once again, read it very carefully. It is far easier to spot mistakes and other shortcomings on a printed document than onscreen. Look out for any factual or word processing errors, or instances of poor presentation, including unrequired or inconsistent:

- variations in size or style of lettering

- headings and subheadings

- numbering

- highlighting techniques

- margins and spacing.

Is every section, subsection, paragraph, sentence and word really necessary? Are they accurate? Do they convey the meaning you intended?

A colleague's check

However, by now you will have read and re-read the draft so often that you may not be able to see the wood for the trees. So ask a sympathetic colleague, who knows as much about the subject as your readers – but not much more – to give his or her candid comments on the amended report. It is far easier to detect flaws in other people's writing than in your own. Are there any obvious errors or ambiguities? What changes or improvements would they suggest? What impact is it likely to have on your readers? You have been too closely involved with the report to assess this objectively.

Your line manager's check

Now pass the further amended report to your line manager. As well as asking the same sort of questions about it as you and your colleague did, your manager will probably be considering wider aspects of the report:

♦ its technical content

♦ its overall relevance

♦ whether it is politically sensitive.

If the report was authorised by a senior officer, your line manager will be particularly concerned that it does credit to the section, firm or profession.

Managers often follow these steps as they appraise draft reports:

♦ **Assimilate**. What is the report trying to achieve? How has the writer attempted to achieve this?

♦ **Question**. Are all the facts, arguments, conclusions and recommendations accurate, complete, convincing and justified? Be prepared to face some very detailed questioning.

♦ **Evaluate**. How significant are the findings?

♦ **Check**. Will the writer need to provide any further evidence or re-assess the practicality of any recommendations? Are all sources properly acknowledged?

♦ **Amend**. Will the report need to be re-structured?

♦ **Edit**. What changes will need to be made to the content or presentation? Are the most important findings, conclusions and recommendations given due prominence? Are less important findings confined to the main body, an appendix, or perhaps omitted?

♦ **Finalise**. Is the report now written to the standard the recipients require, or, in an organisation with many levels of management, to the standard other senior levels require?

If everything is now considered satisfactory, the section and paragraph headings can be finalised, all paragraph and report references checked or amended, the pages numbered, the frontispiece drawn up and, if necessary, an index compiled.

You should be given the opportunity to discuss the reasons for any changes made by your line manager. If this does *not* happen:

♦ You may feel that this is no more than unjustified criticism.

♦ You will not learn from the experience as you can only guess what was wrong with your version.

♦ You may conclude that there is no point in spending so much effort on subsequent reports if they are going to be re-written by superiors.

By now this draft will have so many comments and amendments on it that it will almost certainly need to be re-printed. This is likely to be the final draft. After three drafts it is probable that the report will not get better anyway. Re-writing to get it right is an excellent practice; re-writing as a matter of course is a very bad and wasteful practice.

Preparing the final version

You should be responsible for preparing the final version. There are three reasons for this:

- It will save your line manager's time.

- It will show that you have grasped any points of criticism.

- It will result in a report written in one style, rather than a patchwork from different hands.

Proofreading

It is essential that reports are carefully proof-checked before they are issued. What does this say?

Paris

in the

the spring

And this?

A

bird

in the

the hand

If you were proofreading, you would be expected to have spotted the extra 'the's.

Now, read the sentence below:

FINISHED FILES ARE THE RE-
SULT OF YEARS OF SCIENTIF-
IC STUDY COMBINED WITH
THE EXPERIENCE OF YEARS.

Go back and count the number of 'F's in the sentence. The answer will be given towards the end of this section.

Here is another little proofreading exercise. How many errors are there in this sentence?

> THIS SENTENCE CONTAINES
> FOUR MISSTAKES.

Again, the answer will be given below.

Spell checkers and grammar checkers
Almost all word processing programs come equipped with a tool for checking both spelling and grammar. However, writers should be wary of the dangers of relying too heavily upon them.

> **Spell cheque will knot fined words witch our miss**
> **used butt spelled rite.**

An ordinary spell checker will find few or no errors in the above sentence. This is because most of them can only detect words which are *spelled* incorrectly – only the most sophisticated programs can detect when they are *used* incorrectly.

The following is just a small sample of commonly confused and misused words that standard spell checkers will not flag up: accept/except; advice/advise; allowed/aloud; fewer/less; formally/formerly; its/it's; maybe/may be; moral/morale; more/most; knew/new; of/off; passed/past; personal/personnel; cite/sight/site; sometime/some time; stationary/stationery; than/then; though/through/thorough; who's/whose; and your/you're.

Stories abound of errors which have occurred through spell checkers not highlighting misused words and through writers uncritically accepting inaccurate changes suggested by them. While many of these tales are no doubt apocryphal, they do remind us – often in an amusing and memorable way – of the limitations of spell checkers.

Apparently an eminent QC once agreed to accept the not-so-learned counsel to replace the words 'sua sponte' (a Latin phrase meaning 'on its motion') with the words 'sea sponge' throughout his report. This led to some very unusual sentences, such as:

> 'A trial court must instruct sea sponge on any defence, including a mistake of fact defence.'

Similarly, a doctor prescribed the following for a patient suffering from severe depression:

> 'Lofepramine 4 times a day.'

His spell checker, not recognising the name of the drug, offered a second opinion, which the doctor readily accepted:

> 'Lovemaking 4 time a day.'

Unfortunately, grammar checkers are also of limited value. This has nothing to do with the technology or software, but rather is caused by the nature of grammar itself. For example, my checker did not detect any problems with the following rambling passage:

> 'It is no wondering that advertisings are bad for company in the UK, Sheffield and Germany. McDonald's and Coca Cola are good brand and Gates do good marketing job in Microsoft.'

Yet when it came upon the perfectly reasonable expression 'not at all', it issued the following advice:

'not at all' – wordy expression. Consider 'not' or 'by no means' instead.

Then, later in the same document, my checker declared:

'by no means' – wordy expression. Consider 'not' or 'not at all' instead.

Therefore, it is always wise to think about any changes suggested, rather than simply accepting them as correct. Spell checkers and grammar checkers are only as good as a writer's ability to use them. However much time and effort are put into researching and writing the report, the required result will not be achieved without sufficient care being devoted to the process of old-fashioned human proofreading. A poorly presented report, full of errors and inconsistencies in layout, has a damaging effect regardless of the quality of the content. Mistakes, therefore, must be identified and corrected; there really is no excuse for failing to do this properly.

Proofreading your own work is difficult and inefficient. Because you are so familiar with the report, you tend to race through and think of the bigger picture – the next report. Someone else who has not been working on the report can give it much fresher and more objective scrutiny.

Here are some useful proofreading techniques:

♦ Print out a copy of the report. Spell checkers and grammar checkers miss things, and people do not read text onscreen with the same diligence as they read from a page.

♦ Use a ruler to slow down your reading and make yourself read line by line.

- Read the report out aloud. This process slows down your reading and makes you listen to how it sounds.

- Read the report backwards. Obviously it will not make sense but it is an excellent way to spot spelling mistakes.

- Limit your proofreading to one small section at a time. Then take a short break before proceeding to the next small section.

- Proofread when you are most fresh. This time may be early in the morning or whenever you feel the most alert.

- Try to proofread when you know you will have peace and quiet and can avoid interruptions from the telephone or visitors.

Now for the answers to those exercises. It is probable that you counted three 'F's, whereas there are actually six. The human brain tends to see the 'F' in 'OF' as a 'V'. The second sentence contains three errors: two spelling mistakes and one false claim about its content.

ISSUING THE REPORT

In some organisations the report would now be issued. In others, the following final steps are taken:

- **Discussion**. The writer discusses his or her findings with the key recipients and confirms the factual accuracy of significant points.

- **Clearing**. Any corrective action is agreed and/or the report is amended in the light of any mistakes or misapprehensions shown to have occurred during the investigation.

- **Circulation**. The revised report, clearly annotated 'Draft' on the cover and on every page, is circulated.

- **Agreeing**. The findings are agreed.

- **Issuing**. The final report is issued.

There are important advantages in following these additional steps:

♦ It paves the way for the recommendations.

♦ It prepares the recipients for any criticisms which may be in the final report.

♦ It enables the writer to adapt the tone and emphasis of the report in the light of the recipients' initial reactions.

♦ It increases the probability that the findings will be accepted if they have been fully discussed and the recipients' views have been taken into account.

♦ It enables the writer to avoid errors and misunderstandings which would otherwise undermine his or her credibility and damage the department's or company's reputation.

The responsibility for final approval of the report often rests with the writer's line manager. Once this approval has been obtained arrange for, or make, the correct number of bound copies, including at least one for file. By publication day the names, addresses and designations of all the recipients should be known and checked. Envelopes, wrappers and labels should have been made up, covering letters or compliments slips prepared to explain why the report has been sent and to provide a contact point (probably you), if further enquiry or comment is desired.

Record full details of all issues in a register and try to ensure that each person receives his or her copy at the same time.

SUMMARY

If sufficient time and thought have been devoted to preparing and planning, and possibly revising, a suitable skeletal framework, and to collecting and handling the information required, writing the report will be reasonably straightforward. You will need to amplify the points in each section of the framework, and 'put flesh on the bones'.

The order of writing and revising is important, and should be:

1. Pre-write (targeting, outlining, structuring, developing and checking).

2. Draft the main body and appendixes, beginning with a section, sub-section or appendix you feel particularly confident about.

3. Review the main body and appendices.

4. Draft the references, conclusions, recommendations, introduction and summary, in that order.

5. Check and amend the report with the assistance of a colleague and your line manager.

6. Issue the report, possibly after discussing, clearing, circulating and agreeing a draft report.

Part Two

The Creative Side
of Report Writing

4
A Style Guide to Good Report Writing

During World War II, the Prime Minister sent this memo to his War Cabinet:

CONCISENESS

To do our work, we all have to read a mass of papers. Nearly all of them are far too long. This wastes time, while energy has to be spent looking for the essential points.

I ask my colleagues and their staff to see to it that their reports are shorter.

The aim should be reports, which set out the main points in a series of short, crisp paragraphs.

If a report relies on detailed analysis of some complicated factors, or on statistics, these should be set out in an appendix.

Let us end such phrases as these:

'It is also of importance to bear in mind the following considerations', or 'Consideration should be given to the possibility of carrying into effect'. Most of these woolly phrases are mere padding, which can be left out altogether, or replaced by a single word. Let us not shrink from using the short expressive phrase, even if it is conversational.

Reports drawn up on the lines I propose may first seem rough as compared with the flat surface of officialese jargon. But the saving in time will be great, while the discipline of setting out the real points concisely will prove an aid to clearer thinking.

Winston Churchill, 9 August 1940

This advice and instruction remains as valuable today as it was over 70 years ago – perhaps even more so.

Chapter 3 took a **clinical** view of report writing (the ordering, classifying and sequencing of a document). This chapter turns to the highly subjective and mentally demanding process of effective written communication, and considers that elusive concept known as **style**.

Style is the most nebulous area of report writing. It is very easy to criticise a writer's style as 'poor' or 'inappropriate'; what is not so easy is to specify the stylistic improvements that should be encouraged. This chapter attempts to do just that under these headings:

- Report style.
- Achieving a good style.
- Choosing your words carefully.
- Principles for effective report writing.

REPORT STYLE

To be completely successful, a report which makes recommendations must ensure that the persons for whom the report is intended:

- Read it without unnecessary delay.
- Understand everything in it without undue effort.
- Accept the facts, findings, conclusions and recommendations.
- Decide to take the action recommended.

Achieving this demands more of you than merely presenting relevant facts accurately. It also demands that you communicate in a way that is both *acceptable* and *intelligible* to the readers. Take a look at Appendix 2 for some examples of how this can be achieved.

Good style

It is not possible to define precisely what good style is. Perhaps the nearest working definition is that good style is the best way to get your message across each time you write. Every situation on which a report is prepared will vary, at least slightly. If this were not so, there would be no need for the report to be written. The expression of every point must therefore be drafted with the new situation in mind. Orthodoxy and imitation (for their own sake) are the refuge of the poor report writer.

A good style in report writing involves constructing sentences and paragraphs in such a way that the message you wish to convey is conveyed accurately and quickly to the reader. This is far more difficult to achieve than many writers realise. Reports abound with sentences which their readers have to read two or three times before they can understand.

Once you have issued the report you have no opportunity, at the time the recipients read it, to explain, expand on, or modify what you have written. You cannot reinforce your message by non-verbal communication (as a speaker can by using gestures, facial expressions, intonations and so on). The readers get no further assistance from you: they have to work on their own to understand what you have said and to fathom your meaning. And, if the report is written in a bad style, the reader may get the wrong meaning, or perhaps no meaning at all. Your constant aim, therefore, should be to make the readers' task easier, and to ensure that what they understand when they read the report is what you *intended* them to understand.

The word 'style' is not used here – as it is normally used in discussing literature – as a term for appraising the quality of a writer's method of expression. A person may be well-educated and write in an excellent literary style, yet use a bad style in writing a report – because he or she fails to *communicate* with the reader. A good style in business communication – unlike a good literary style – should combine:

- ◆ clarity
- ◆ conciseness
- ◆ and directness.

In a report the style of writing should be *unobtrusive*; if the reader becomes aware of the style of writing it probably means that the writing is pompous, or ostentatious, or ambiguous, or difficult to follow. Above all else, the writing should be easy to read. Good style is good manners.

Research into what makes a piece of writing readable started in America over seventy years ago. Experts nowadays agree that the factors that most affect readability are:

- ◆ an attractive appearance
- ◆ non-technical subject matter
- ◆ a clear and direct style
- ◆ short sentences
- ◆ short and familiar words.

ACHIEVING A GOOD STYLE

Your style of dress is different on a beach, at a wedding and at work. Similarly, your style of writing should be different on a postcard, in a prepared wedding speech and in a report.

There are certain conventions within the field of report writing. For example, reports should always be **serious** (concerned with important matters) without ever becoming **solemn** (gloomy and sombre). However, a writer should be given as much freedom as possible within these conventions. This encourages the development of a natural, less inhibited writing style which, in turn, leads to better report writing.

There are numerous ways in which you can bring individuality to whatever you write, which will not only enable you to communicate more effectively, but also give your writing extra colour and impact.

Selectivity

Careful choice of words can enable you to convey many subtleties of meaning. You cannot find a word you have forgotten or do not know in a dictionary. Look up a word of similar meaning in a **thesaurus** and you will find a variety of words and expressions which should include the one in the back of your mind, or perhaps an even more appropriate one which you had not even considered.

Accuracy

Check that everything you write is factually accurate. The facts should be capable of being verified. Moreover, arguments should be soundly based and your reasoning should be logical. You should not write anything that will misinform, mislead or unfairly persuade your readers. If you do, you will be doing a disservice not only to yourself but also to your department and organisation. Accurate information is essential for effective communication and decision making.

It is sometimes tempting to take short-cuts. If you are writing as a specialist for non-specialists you may feel that you can make statements which you would not make for a technical readership, in order to press a case. The danger with such an approach is that you only have to be found out once for your entire credibility to be destroyed, or at the very least undermined.

There is an old saying that liars must have good memories. In any case, it is much easier to write honestly and fairly. This makes for an enhanced personal reputation, and a growing confidence in the reliability of your findings, conclusions and recommendations.

Objectivity

A report should not be an essay reflecting personal emotions and opinions. You must look at all sides of a problem with an open mind before stating your conclusions. The role is similar to that of a sports referee or a High Court judge. In these situations, decisions are based on the results, the evidence, or an interpretation of the evidence – not on personal opinions and feelings.

Making it clear that you have an open mind when writing your report will, in most cases, make your conclusions and recommendations more acceptable to your readers. The emphasis, therefore, should be on the factual material presented and the conclusions drawn, rather than on any personal beliefs, biases or prejudices.

Conciseness

Veni, Vidi, Vici (I came, I saw, I conquered). That is how Julius Caesar reported his visit to our shores. While none of your reports will be as short as this, you should aim to keep them concise. In doing this, do not mistake brevity for conciseness. A report may be brief because it omits important information. A concise report, on the other hand, is short but still contains all the essential details.

To ensure you do not include material which can safely be left out, you should *not* ask: 'Can this information be included?' Rather, you *should* ask: 'Is it *necessary* for this information to be included?' In this way, you will be sure to put into your report only as much information as your readers need in order to respond as you wish them to.

Several software grammar-checkers aspire to provide general advice on conciseness. These include Gunning's *Fog Index*, Flesch's *Reading Ease Score*, Fry's *Readability Graph* and Morris's *Clear River Test*. While they all have at least something to offer, they disregard such things as the use of actives and passives, the way the information is organised, how it looks on a page, and the reader's motivation and level of prior knowledge. They give only the merest hint about how to write better text and they encourage the idea that a clear document is one that scores well on a formula. Few serious writers bother to use them.

While it may be a truism, keeping the average length of sentences short is one of the best ways of ensuring conciseness. Aim for an average sentence length of less than 20 words. This does not mean, of course, that every sentence in a section must contain no more than 20 words. In fact, it is preferable to vary the lengths and constructions of sentences, otherwise your writing will have a staccato rhythm or a terseness which many readers may find either childish or otherwise irritating. (That sentence has 34 words.)

Clarity and consistency

The best way to achieve clarity in your writing is to allow some time to elapse between the first draft and its revision. Try to leave it over the weekend, or at least overnight. If you are really under pressure and this is simply not possible, at least leave it over a lunch or coffee break. It is essential to have a period of time, no matter how short, when you can think of other things. In this way, when you come back to the report, you can look at it with a degree of objectivity.

You can, however, increase your chances of writing with clarity and consistency if, as you write, you try to keep certain things in mind. Concentrate on a mental picture of your readers, and make sure you are writing for them and not for yourself.

Simplicity

Usually, if your writing is selective, accurate, objective, concise, clear and consistent, it will also be as simple as it can be. You should guard against over-simplifying, for example to the point of missing out information which the reader needs to fully understand what you are trying to say. You should again keep your readers firmly in mind and keep asking yourself whether or not they will be able to follow the logic of your presentation.

Many problems in communicating are caused by making things more difficult than they need to be. Many writers also over-estimate the reading capacity of the report's recipients. They forget, or do not know, that the average manager has a reading speed of about 225 words per minute and comprehends only about 75 per cent of what is read. That is why the summary is so important. Even if recipients are going to read the whole report, the summary tells them the essential points being made. It is always easier for readers to process information when they have some knowledge of it in advance. Again remember the adage: tell them what you are going to say, then say it, then tell them what you said.

Keeping technical writing simple

The problem of how to keep things simple is particularly acute for technical writers. The information they have to convey is difficult for non-technical readers to understand. If they simplify their expression too much they may distort the meaning of whatever they are trying to say. It is all too easy for them to shrug their shoulders and tell themselves that it is not their fault and their readers will just have to follow them the best they can.

This simply will not do. The readers, after all, are the really important people. If they do not understand, they will reject what the writer has to say. If the writer depends on their approval for a course of action, he or she is helping no one by refusing to take their limitations into account. No writer can afford to be so self-indulgent.

Benefits of simplicity

The rewards of writing simply are considerable. Readers will at least *understand* what has been said and will be more likely to respond favourably to conclusions drawn and recommendations made. They will form a higher opinion of the writer and they will read subsequent reports with greater attention and enthusiasm.

CHOOSING YOUR WORDS CAREFULLY

When children are learning English at school, they are encouraged to use longer and longer words in progressively more complex sentences. Paradoxically, the report writer should be encouraged to do just the opposite. Generally, prefer short words in short sentences: the right word, however modest, is never undignified.

Prefer plain words

Do not be afraid of plain English. Write to express, not to impress. Prefer words your readers are likely to understand.

not   The ready availability of computer-based tutorials associated with applications software has become prevalent since the development of Microsoft Windows.

but   Computer-based tutorials associated with applications software have become readily available since the development of Microsoft Windows.

In 2009, MPs on the House of Commons' select committee for monitoring the Department for Innovation, Universities and Skills criticised its civil servants for using 'jargon-riddled phrases' and 'euphemisms deflecting likely failure', quoting a section of the department's annual report which stated that they faced a 'challenging growth strategy for 2010'; that is, they were unlikely to meet targets.

Another bizarre use of obscure language cited from the report was this sentence (if, indeed, it *is* a sentence):

> 'An overarching national improvement strategy which drives up quality and performance underpinned by specific plans for strategically significant areas of activity, such as workforce and technology.'

Not surprisingly, officials were reminded to use plain English.

In the same year, Lord Jackson's report, 'Review of Civil Litigation Costs' contained this baffling observation:

> 'Personal injuries litigation is the paradigm instance of litigation in which the parties are in an asymmetric relationship.'

As the Plain English Campaign points out, perhaps Lord Jackson could have said:

> 'Personal injuries cases are examples of court cases between different parties.'

If you find yourself about to write a word that you would not use in everyday conversation, ask yourself: 'Do I *really* need to use this word?' The overuse of uncommon words will make your report seem pompous, officious and long-winded. Not that anyone should forbid you from ever using them, but judicious use of the alternatives will make your report shorter, simpler and more conversational in style.

Avoid pointless words

Some words and phrases – like *basically, actually, undoubtedly, each and every one* and *during the course of our investigation* – keep cropping up in reports. Yet they add nothing to the message and often can be removed without changing the meaning or the tone. Try leaving them out of your writing. You will find your sentences survive, succeed and may even flourish without them.

Avoid overwriting and padding

Weed out any meaningless, excess words.

> *not*   Accounts Receivable is not concerned with the follow-up of any of the items with the exception of delinquent accounts.
>
> *but*   Accounts Receivable follows up delinquent accounts only.

Avoid redundant words

Repetition of a word can keep the reader aware of the topic. However, saying the same thing twice over in different words for no good reason is tautology.

> *not*   Past history suggests that our future prospects are bright.
>
> *but*   History suggests that our prospects are bright.

Avoid the careless positioning of words

This can cause misunderstanding and confusion.

> *not*   The headteacher was urged to take a strong line on absenteeism by the board of governors.
>
> *but*   The board of governors urged the headteacher to take a strong line on absenteeism.

Prefer the positive
Try to use positive statements wherever possible.

not   We do not believe the backup files are adequate.

but   We believe the backup files are inadequate.

Try to avoid qualifying introductions
Readers, seeing a qualification, are put on notice that they must keep this in mind until they read the rest of the report. This irritates.

not   While repayment of these amounts is provided for, the ten per cent interest is not included.

but   Repayment of these amounts is provided for, but the ten per cent interest is not included.

Place emphasis at the end of the sentence
The strength of a sentence is at its end.

not   With a little clarification, the subcontractor would have solved the difficulties occasioned by the specification changes more readily.

but   With a little clarification, the subcontractor would more readily have solved the difficulties occasioned by the specification changes.

Prefer English to foreign words and phrases
Using uncommon foreign-language terms like *inter alia*, *per se*, and *sine die* may look like showing off. Avoid them unless there are no good English equivalents – and unless you are *sure* that your audience will understand them.

Avoid sexist language
The tone of your writing should not reflect a gender bias – or any other bias, such as race, religion, age or disability. Such writing can

send the wrong or hidden message and may alienate readers. While an awareness of the need to avoid sexual discrimination in writing goes back many decades, it was in the 1980s that acceptance of this need became widespread. Impetus was given by the increase in the number of women in the workplace and today many schools and colleges teach non-sexist writing.

The use of pronouns in a sentence where the gender of the noun has not been revealed is often perceived as sexist, whether intentional or not. For example, if you use personal pronouns referring to a manager as 'he' and a personal assistant as 'she', you are stereotyping. You can avoid this by omitting pronouns, changing to the plural form when possible, or by using both genders.

not   A good manager will gain the respect of his staff.
but   A good manager will gain the respect of staff.

not   A personal assistant should be loyal to her boss.
but   Personal assistants should be loyal to their bosses.

not   A report writer should get to know his readers.
but   A report writer should get to know his or her readers.

Various words and expressions can also be perceived as indicating a gender bias. With a little thought, it is possible to use more acceptable alternatives.

not   policeman,   *but*   police officer
not   fireman,   *but*   fire fighter
not   businessman,   *but*   businessperson.

However, it is not easy to prepare a long report which is entirely gender-neutral. To do so tends to produce immoderately long sentences, excessive use of the passive and, sometimes, ambiguous writing. Also, it seems reasonable that where there is an overwhelming majority of one sex in the report's readership, the use of pronouns should reflect this.

Use warm words

Words are powerful. They conjure up images, evoke emotions and trigger responses deep within us so that we react, often without knowing why. So-called *warm* words make us feel secure and comfortable, while *cold* words leave us uneasy and unsure. Writer Henry James said the two most beautiful words in the English language are *summer afternoon* because they evoke just the right emotions.

In the early days of instant coffee, advertisers got off to a bad start by stressing words like *quick*, *time-saving* and *efficient*. These are all words without warmth and feeling. Makers of fresh coffee fought back with warm, happy, appetising words like *aroma*, *fresh* and *tasty*. Makers of instant coffee soon learned the lesson and their product became *delicious*, *rich* and *satisfying*. Sales *blossomed*. The rest, as they say, is history.

Once you get into the habit of looking at the emotional colouring of words, as well as their meanings, you will find yourself using the kind of language that puts readers at ease and causes them to react more favourably to your reports and to you.

PRINCIPLES FOR EFFECTIVE REPORT WRITING

There are several well-known and well-tested pieces of advice to people who wish to communicate effectively on paper. Here are some that should prove particularly valuable to report writers.

The importance of reports

The report is the major product of your project or investigation. Indeed, for most people it is the only tangible evidence that any work has been undertaken. It should not be silent on all your hard work. There is as much importance in presenting facts as in finding them; what is not reported will soon be forgotten, and might as well never have been discovered.

Drafting the report

♦   Try to write your draft report over consecutive days. You will find that in two days you will achieve three times what you can in one; in four days you will do four times what you might in two.

♦   Write in bursts of about 40 minutes to an hour, each followed by a short break.

♦   Never start a writing session without being clear what you intend to achieve.

♦   Be flexible. You may have to postpone a writing session to do some other work. However, flexibility works both ways, so make the most of any unexpected writing opportunities.

♦   A ten-minute solo walk can often be more useful than an hour sitting at your desk.

♦   Once you have started, keep the momentum going. Do not be over-concerned with writing conventions at this stage. There will be time for this later.

♦   Read a passage aloud to yourself. If it sounds like the latest news from the Middle East, or staccato or complicated, you are failing.

The need for explanation

♦   Always begin by saying what you have been asked to do, who asked you and when. Say how, where and when you did it, and with whose help. Always explain what you are talking about. Never be afraid of explaining too much.

- Try to consolidate highly factual reference into self-contained sections which will be seen as help for those who require it, but not as required reading for those who do not.

- Always make it clear what you have accepted, and what you have verified. When you have verified something, say how.

- You cannot explain the present without first explaining the past. Begin at the beginning. How do things come to be where they are now?

- Be specific. Words like 'mostly', 'largely' and 'substantially' merely raise the question 'how much?'. Say instead 'three-quarters', 'two-thirds', 'about half'; there is no need to be finicky, but you must say what you mean.

Differentiating between important facts and details

The best report writers are those who know which are the main facts, and which are the details that illustrate them. If you did not fully understand that sentence, please read it again. It is possibly the most important there is in this book.

Avoiding too many figures

A common mistake in writing reports is to produce too many figures and too few explanations. The principles to follow are two-fold:

- Restrict figures to those which are meaningful.

- Make sure they are consistently produced and interpreted.

Never assume that the readers will draw the right conclusion from the figures. They may quite easily not be reading them at all when they read the text; or they may read them and make the wrong conclusion; or they may fail to make any conclusion. Always say in words what they mean.

Layout

Be consistent:

♦ Do not change names or descriptions without good reason. For example, if you describe a unit in the main body as 'the manufacturing department', do not refer to it as 'the factory' in the summary.

♦ Write dates the same way throughout (6th December 2012, or perhaps December 6, 2012).

♦ The numbers one to ten look better in words, larger numbers look better in figures.

♦ The layout of headings, pages and paragraphs should not vary.

Keep cross-references to a minimum. Wherever possible exhaust a topic the first time it comes up. If something does have to be mentioned in two places, give the reference to the first discussion the second time you deal with it, not vice-versa. To be told that something is going to come up again casts doubt on what you have just read. Cross-reference to part and section numbers, not to pages or paragraphs; the parts of the draft report already revised can then be typed in final form before the later parts are finished.

SUMMARY

Style is an elusive concept. Perhaps the nearest we can get to a working definition is that good style is the best way to get your message across each time you write. Your aim should be to write reports which are:

♦ read without unnecessary delay

♦ understood without undue effort

♦ accepted and, where appropriate, acted upon.

Research has suggested that the factors that most affect readability are:

♦ An attractive appearance.

♦ Non-technical subject-matter.

♦ A clear and direct style.

♦ Short sentences.

♦ Short, familiar words.

There are numerous ways in which you can bring individuality to whatever you write, which will not only enable you to communicate more effectively, but also give your writing extra colour and impact. It should be selective, accurate, objective, concise, clear, consistent and simple.

A report is an important document.

♦ Draft it in short, concentrated bursts.

♦ Pay particular attention to the need for explanation.

♦ Differentiate between important facts and details.

♦ Avoid too many figures.

♦ Be consistent throughout.

5
The Correct Use of English

In report writing accuracy and precision are essential. Your writing must be concise, unambiguous and authoritative – and yet attractive to read. If it is not, this will reflect badly on you. At best your reports will be vague and misleading; at worst they will be confusing and inaccurate. You do not need to have an extensive knowledge of the correct use of English, but you do need to know the basic rules.

This chapter considers the importance of accurate and precise:

♦   Grammar

♦   Punctuation

♦   Spelling.

Let us consider each in turn.

GRAMMAR

Writers often look at their work and have an uneasy feeling that it is not quite right, but do not know why. Understanding the basic rules of grammar helps identify the malady and its root cause. The cure then presents itself. Here are some rules that may be of help to you:

Rule	Example
Tense and Person	
1. Reports are normally written in the simple past tense. What you must decide is whether it should be in the first or third person; the first person is personal, the third impersonal. It is generally regarded as more professional to write in the third person, thereby avoiding the pronouns 'I' and 'we'.	*First person singular:* I recommend . . . *First person plural:* We recommend . . . *Third person:* It is recommended . . .
Paragraph construction	
1. A paragraph should read as complete in itself.	
2. Its sentences should vary in length.	
3. It should begin with a topic sentence.	The main reason why people want to work is to earn money.
4. The remainder of the paragraph should 'fill out' the topic sentence.	
5. The paragraph should contain only information relevant to the topic sentence.	
6. The final sentence should sum up that paragraph and link to the next.	While financial incentive provides strong motivation, it is not the only reason why people want to work.
Sentence construction	
1. A sentence is a set of words complete in itself as an expression of thought.	

2.	Generally, keep sentences as short and simple as possible. However, their length and complexity should be varied to maintain interest.	Jesus wept. (John 11:35)
3.	Every sentence should have one main assertion. The normal construction is subject – verb – object (or complement).	The woman reviewed the report.
4.	Words should be in a logical order.	The report will be issued next week. *not* Issuing of the report will take place next week.
5.	Generally, prefer the active voice to the passive voice	Stephen wrote the report. *is better than* The report was written by Stephen.
6.	However, if you want to say something is being done, passive is more natural.	The audit will be take place next week.
7.	Also, passive is better when the result is more important than the action.	The report has been printed.
8.	Use the passive voice where the doer is obvious or unknown.	The office was burgled during the early hours of Monday morning.
9.	The passive is also useful to avoid the continual repetition of I/we.	It was discovered that . . .
10.	Use the passive voice when writing up an experiment.	A glass stopper was weighed.
11.	The first and last words of a sentence get more attention than those in the middle.	Effective report writing requires a systematic approach, as most people appreciate. *is stronger than* Effective report writing, as most people appreciate, requires a systematic approach.

12. The word order can change the emphasis or meaning of a sentence.	She reads only on Fridays. *means she does not read on any other day.* She only reads on Fridays. *means she does nothing but read on Fridays.*
13. Always remember the subject of the sentence.	The report highlights several weaknesses in managerial control. The situation has not improved since the last audit. *is better than* The report highlights several weaknesses in managerial control and has not improved since the last audit. *This says the report (the subject) has not improved.*

Phrases and Clauses

1. Avoid unnecessary phrases and clauses.	*Use* Obviously *not* It is obvious that.
2. A positive sentence is easier to read than a qualified one.	Most of the errors had been corrected but two have not been. *is better than* While most of the errors had been corrected, two had not been.
3. Where phrases are used, they should follow the subject. A qualifying phrase can be removed without ruining the sentence.	Stephen, who works in the accounts department, wrote the report.

Numbers

1. Use words for numbers up to ten.	The report assesses four proposals.
2. Use figures for numbers over ten.	The company has 614 employees.
3. Use figures in a listing which contains both large and small numbers.	The committee consists of 4 men and 16 women.

4.	Spell it out if the number is the first word of a sentence.	Eighty-one complaints were received.
5.	Use figures to express sums of money.	£5,000,000 or £5 million.
6.	Use figures to record chapter and page numbers – and when referring to sections and paragraphs of a report.	Chapter 2, page 53; III.2.4; 4.2.2.
7.	Use figures to express decimals, dimensions, weights, temperatures and percentages.	5.9, 16cm x 23cm, 4 kilos, 15°C, 28 per cent (in the text) or 28% (in statistical tables and illustrations).
8.	Use words to express numbers that are approximate.	The petition contained about two thousand signatures. *but* The petition contained 2016 signatures.
9.	Use figures to represent time.	14.00 hrs or 2.00pm.

PUNCTUATION

The purpose of punctuation is simply to make it easier for the reader to understand the text. A good way to check your punctuation is to read aloud. Whenever you pause or change the inflexion of your voice, you should use some form of punctuation mark. But which? The answer obviously is important. If you use the wrong one, or put it in the wrong place, you can give a sentence a meaning which you did not intend. Consider the following eight words when punctuated in different ways:

> The man said the woman was a fool.
> 'The man,' said the woman, 'was a fool.'
> The man said, 'The woman was a fool.'

The first sentence gives the *reported* speech of the *man*; the second gives the *actual* speech of the wo*man*; the third gives the *actual* speech of the *man*.

The following basic rules will help you to decide which punctuation marks you should use, and where you should use them:

Rule	Example
1. Use a capital letter to start the first word of a sentence. Also use them for people's names, place names and titles. Most report writers also use capitals for indexes and section headings. Problems occur in headings which are a mixture of capitals and lower case letters, but the basic rule is to use capitals for the first letter of each word which is not either a preposition or a conjunction.	Gordon Beadon; London; Lord High Chancellor; Department for Work and Pensions; 'Absenteeism at ABC Limited, 2001–2010'.
2. Use a full stop (.) to end a sentence. Also use them after each letter which represents a word in an abbreviation.	E.F.C., European Forestry Commission (*three words*). Nat. Hist., Natural History (*two words*). Km., kilometre (*one word*).
3. Use a comma (,) to separate three or more items in a list.	We considered glass, plastic, polythene and polystyrene.
4. Use a comma to represent a pause in a sentence.	The report, which was written by Stephen, will be issued next week.
5. Use a comma to differentiate between clauses that define and those that comment.	Mr Jones who was elected chairperson takes over from Mr Smith on Tuesday. (*definition*) Mr Jones, who was elected chairperson, takes over from Mr Smith on Tuesday. (*comment*)

6. Use a semi-colon (;) instead of a full stop to join 'sentences' or clauses which have some bearing on each other.	England won the Ashes in 2011; it was their first series victory on Australian soil for 24 years.
7. Use a semi-colon to mark off phrases (especially lists) in which a comma already appears.	The men worked in the fields; the women, in the factory; the children, in the school.
8. Use a colon (:) to represent 'that is to say' or 'namely', before providing a list.	There are many sources of information: people, books and other publications, information available electronically and events and places.
9. Use a colon to introduce an explanatory statement.	This is our decision: to accept the offer and sell the factory.
10. Use a colon to introduce a quotation where a comma already appears in the sentence.	Referring to her notes, she said: 'I visited the office on 16th September.'
11. Use dashes (–) instead of brackets to indicate parenthesis. Dashes are stronger than a pair of commas but weaker than brackets.	The athletes – there were ten of them – all completed the race.
12. Use a dash to indicate an additional thought.	Clegg came to this month's meeting – it was the first he had attended since April.
13. Use a dash where a word is repeated, together with an explanation or with elaboration.	We need to win the match today – and to win it by at least three goals.
14. Use an apostrophe (') to shorten a word. Place it above the space created by the removal of the letter. Such contractions are not usual in formal writing.	is not – isn't do not – don't
15. Use an apostrophe to indicate possession. If the word requiring the apostrophe is singular, place it before the 's'; if it is plural, place it after the 's'.	Britain's voters (*the voters of Britain*). Teachers' unions (*unions of teachers*).

16. Do not use apostrophes with possessive pronouns or where they are otherwise not required.	hers *not* her's its *not* it's giros *not* giro's
17. Use inverted commas ('...') immediately before and after direct speech or a quotation.	As Wellington said, 'publish and be damned.'
18. Use single and double inverted commas where there is a quotation within direct speech.	He said: 'As Henry Ford remarked, "you can have any colour so long as it's black."'
19. Use inverted commas where a word is used 'oddly'.	A semi-colon can be used to join 'sentences' which have some bearing on each other. *Inverted commas are used because they are no longer separate sentences.*
20. Do not use inverted commas when stating facts.	Everest is the highest mountain in the world. *This statement does not require inverted commas.*
21. Use a question mark (?) at the end of a sentence containing a query.	That is quite straightforward, isn't it?
22. Use an exclamation mark (!) to suggest a sudden change of emotion. Use them sparingly; they rarely appear in reports.	You must be joking!
23. Use brackets ( ) to enclose explanatory words.	Report writers must be aware of the main principles of the law of libel (defamation published in a permanent form).

SPELLING

To many people, incorrect spelling indicates carelessness and a lack of attention to detail. This impression must be avoided. You should therefore have a good dictionary and always refer to it if you are unsure about a word's spelling, or about its precise meaning or usage. The dangers of relying too heavily upon a spell checker were highlighted on page 69. You need to establish the correct spelling from the context.

Try to identify words that you often struggle with and then find ways to help remember how to spell them. For example:

Accommodation – 'Two double rooms, please.' *Reminds you that it has two double letters.*
Cemetery – Ghosts go 'eee!'
Necessary – A jacket has one collar and two sleeves. *One C and two Ss.*

English is derived from a number of different sources – Norman French, Anglo-Saxon, Greek, Latin, Norse – with Arab, Indian, African and other influences. So the rules of much of English spelling are not easy or consistent, as the following anonymous poem reminds us:

> Beware of heard, a dreadful word,
> That looks like beard and sounds like bird,
> And dead: it's said like bed, not bead,
> For Goodness sake, don't call it deed!
> Watch out for meat and great and threat.
> They rhyme with suite and straight and debt.

However, here are some general rules and guidelines that should help:

Rule	Example
1. Be careful not to omit part of a word.	accidentally *not* accidently
2. Do not join up two separate words.	in fact *not* infact a lot *not* alot
3. 'I' before 'e', except after 'c'.	field, yield, receive. However, be wary of some weird exceptions: neither, either, leisure
4. The prefix 'dis' is not hyphenated.	discontinue *not* dis-continue
5. The prefix 'sub' is not normally hyphenated.	subeditor *not* sub-editor
6. The prefix 'un' is not normally hyphenated.	uncertified *not* un-certified
7. You do not normally change the spelling of a word when adding a prefix to it.	mis + spell = misspell
8. To form the plural of words ending in 'y': If there is a consonant immediately before the 'y' in the singular, then the plural is 'ies'. If there is a vowel immediately before the 'y' in the singular, then the plural is 'ys'.	lady – ladies valley – valleys
9. Pay particular attention to words which are pronounced the same, or very similarly, but are spelt differently (homophones).	there, their and they're to, two and two

SUMMARY

You cannot express yourself accurately and precisely without knowing and applying the basic rules of grammar and punctuation and spelling.

Keep things as simple as possible, without ever oversimplifying. Your aim is to communicate effectively, not to win any literary prizes. Whenever possible choose familiar words, in short sentences within short paragraphs. However, always use language that conveys the precise meaning you wish to deliver – and don't forget to check your spelling.

Finally – and by way of a little light relief – here are 20 statements, each of which is itself a demonstration of the fault it describes:

♦ First and foremost, avoid clichés like the plague.

♦ A verb have to agree with its subject.

♦ There is no excuse for incorect spelling.

♦ Avoid abstract nouns, in truth they are not readily understood.

♦ Never use no double negatives.

♦ It makes sense not to use the same words in two senses in the same sentence.

♦ It is pathetic and criminal to use emotive language.

♦ Place pronouns as close as possible, especially in long sentences, to their antecedents.

♦ 'Avoid the overuse of "quotation marks".'

♦ Avoid all un-necessary hyphens.

♦ Use commas only, when necessary.

♦ Do not overuse exclamation marks!!!

♦ Don't use contractions in formal writing.

♦ Always avoid all awkward and affected alliteration.

♦ Avoid using the same word over and over and over again.

- Verily it is incumbent upon thee to avoid ensamples of archaic words.

- Avoid mixed metaphors; with enough time on your hands you should never end up with egg on your face.

- Having drafted the report, all dangling principles must be deleted.

- Make sure you never a word out.

- *Le mot de la fin*: do not use foreign words or phrases if there are good English equivalent words or phrases.

6
Improving the Presentation of Your Report

Technology provides new, exciting and better ways of improving the presentation of a report. A computer equipped with word processing or desktop publishing software not only makes the work easier but also provides the opportunity for you to create a report every bit as polished and professional as one produced by an expert team including a writer, typist, typesetter and graphic artist.

The differences between word processing and desktop publishing (DTP) are fading. Word processing can be used to design documents. Desktop publishing can be used for ordinary, simple documents as well as highly sophisticated publications. Today, the two areas overlap extensively and are frequently used interchangeably.

The objectives of good presentation are:

- To attract and retain the interest of the readers.
- To help them understand the contents of the report without undue effort.
- To enable them to find their way around the report quickly.
- To demonstrate your professionalism and, where appropriate, that of your department and/or your organisation.

Word processing or desktop publishing software can help you achieve these objectives. Unless you are using a steam-driven PC, you will be able to work *wysiwyg*. Pronounced *whizzywig*, this acronym stands for *what you see is what you get*. In most applications what you see onscreen is an accurate representation of how the document you are working on will print out. This means you can adjust the appearance of your report, making revisions to the look, until you are completely happy with the result.

This chapter provides a guide to determining the appearance of your report. It begins with an overview of what word processing and desktop publishing can do for the report writer. Then it considers how this technology can be used most effectively to enhance each of the four elements which collectively create a high quality, professional-looking report, namely:

♦ layout and design

♦ typography

♦ illustrations

♦ colour.

Finally, it looks at other ways of making a report stand out from the pack, through careful choice of paper, covers, binding and indexing.

Let us begin with the overview.

WORD PROCESSING AND DESKTOP PUBLISHING

Flexibility is the key attribute of word processing and desktop publishing. Once you have got your text onscreen, you can edit it, format it, save your work as a file and print it out. Whole blocks of text can be inserted or deleted in the middle of a report with everything else moving around to accommodate the changes. Paragraphs can be shifted from one section of a report to another. Sentences can be amended. Words can be highlighted. In short, you can do pretty much what you like with it.

As well as providing basic tools for drawing line rules, boxes and other embellishments, most word processors allow graphics and tabular information to be imported from other programs – including accounts packages and spreadsheets that can prepare charts and tables from the data they hold.

If you have standard reports that need to be revised each time they are used, you can create them as templates, then personalise copies just before they are printed without the need to retype from scratch or take the unprofessional-looking route of typing or writing onto a photocopied standard report. Facilities for numbering pages and providing headers and footers can be found in most word processors. These automate repetitive processes.

On the design front, you can expect **style** functions that allow you to save the attributes of text – font, size, colour and so on – as a style you can apply easily to sections of text you highlight using the mouse. This facility helps to keep consistency both within a report and between reports. You can change the fonts that you use in a report at will, providing you have installed fonts under your operating system.

You may wish to consider add-on packages in order to improve the more popular word processing software. Task-specific programs that help you structure, say, a marketing plan can help you and your word processor enter into new fields by providing the examples and expertise needed to create detailed and competent reports.

There are numerous business-specific applications that are designed to address particular sectors of commerce or industry, which are referred to as 'vertical' applications. Some can be applied generally, such as Computer Aided Design (CAD) packages, but many are only relevant to one field – estate agency, insurance or the like. Buying programs of this nature is a complex subject, as your own requirements may in reality be quite different from someone working in a different area of the same profession. If you are looking for a solution of this kind, then you should get in contact with your professional body or institute, which will maintain a list of recognised software suppliers. It will sometimes be able to make specific recommendations as to which package will be best for you, but more likely will leave the research side up to you.

Checklist: word processing and desktop publishing

♦ Don't worry about your typing speed. Most two-finger typists can type faster than they think, and with practice your speed will improve.

♦ Unless you are a graphic designer or have a real need to produce documents for professional printing, you are unlikely to need the facilities of high-end desktop publishing.

♦ Talk to other people who use word processors and see how they use the features their program offers.

♦ Consider setting up a 'house-style' to use in your report, keeping the number of fonts to a minimum but using standard, attractive layouts. A set of templates can then be used as the starting point for all your reports.

♦ Develop a filing system on your computer so you can easily find and reload reports. If you are dealing with a large number of reports, check that your word processor can search by summary information or the content of a report, rather than just the filename under which reports have been saved.

LAYOUT AND DESIGN

Many considerations and decisions are required when choosing your overall layout and design. In particular, you will need to think about:

♦ format

♦ page size and orientation

♦ margins and spacing

♦ headings and subheadings

♦ numbering.

Format

Reports of today do not have to look like the traditional reports of yesterday. They can *look* interesting and make people *want* to read them. Word processing and desktop publishing techniques can be used to create new, reader-friendly reports in exciting formats such as modern, ultra-modern and enhanced modern.

A **traditional** report is the kind that used to be produced on a typewriter. A **modern** report takes this format one stage further by adding lines and boxes, changing font sizes and using italics. An **ultra-modern** report has the additional feature of a two- or three-column format. People read faster and comprehend more information when reading short rather than long lines of text. In an **enhanced modern** report, images are added and manipulated. This is an excellent format for reports because people are used to reading newspapers, journals and magazines presented in this way.

Figure 5 illustrates three designs which offer possible starting points for creating your own page layouts.

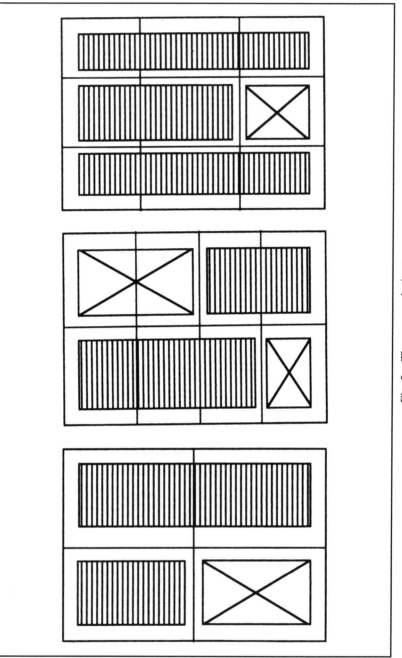

Fig. 5. Three page designs.

Throughout the remainder of this chapter you will find everything you need to know to be able to create a professional report in any format. If you choose a traditional **single-column** layout, it is advisable to use 12-point type. A variation to this is to use just one column but to shorten the line length. This not only makes the material easier and faster to read, but also allows space for artwork, graphics, captions, headings and subheadings. The use of **two-** or even **three-column** formats gives a report a very professional look and increases the readability of copy. Smaller 9-, 10-, or 11-type size is recommended.

Page size and orientation

What size of paper will you use? The standard pages are these:

Paper size	mm	inches
A1	594 x 841	23.4 x 33.1
A2	420 x 594	16.5 x 23.4
A3	297 x 420	11.7 x 16.5
A4	210 x 297	8.3 x 11.7
A5	148 x 210	5.8 x 8.3

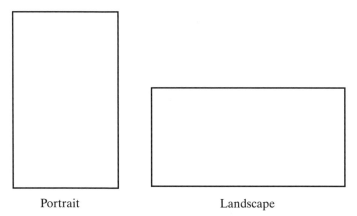

Portrait   Landscape

Fig. 6.   Page orientation.

Writers tend to choose standard A4 paper as a matter of course. However, at least consider other options. If you are using a photocopier or laser printer, make sure the paper you choose will go through your machine.

In addition to size of paper, you will need to think about its orientation (see Figure 6). Will the report be portrait (vertical/tall) or landscape (horizontal/wide)? Most reports are portrait. Consider whether a landscape orientation for your report might work even more effectively.

Margins and spacing

It is far easier for a reader to assimilate information presented in small sections than in huge, uninterrupted blocks of print. Pages with too much type and artwork give the appearance of being too heavy and hard to read. **White space** (or whatever colour background is used) is very important not only to help the reader, but also to give the report a professional look. It is important to allow:

♦ Adequate space between the lines of print (reports are often double-spaced with 1½-spacing for sub-paragraphs).

♦ An adequate and consistent margin on the left of the page for binding (the size of margin on the left will vary according to the type of binding selected).

♦ Clear and consistent gaps between sections and paragraphs.

♦ A margin of at least an inch at the top (the header zone) and bottom (the footer zone) of the page.

Using short bulleted lists of related items (such as the one above) is another good way of breaking up paragraphs of text to make it easier to read. The list may be introduced by a colon, a dash, or both (:-), and the size of any indentations must be consistent.

Headings and subheadings

Headings and subheadings help busy readers of today by identifying and labelling blocks of type. They are not standard. You must invent them. Make sure that they:

◆ are comparatively short

◆ are descriptive

◆ would be expected, or at least would be easily interpreted

◆ cover all the ground (collectively)

◆ do not overlap (although the same information may appear under more than one heading if it supports more than one argument)

◆ are never vague (for example, avoid headings such as 'General', 'Miscellaneous' and 'Other')

◆ are in an order which readers will find logical (perhaps in alphabetical order, in chronological order, or in order of importance)

◆ are identical to those listed in the table of contents (if used).

Once you have introduced a topic with a heading or subheading, you cannot leave that topic and move on to another one until you provide another heading or subheading. For this reason subheadings should not repeat information provided in headings. For example, if your heading is 'ABC Limited', your subheadings could be 'Production Department', 'Accounts Department' and 'Personnel Department'. There is no need to write, 'ABC Limited – Production Department'.

Remember that the title of the report should be more prominent than section headings; section headings more prominent than paragraph headings; paragraph headings more prominent than sub-paragraph headings, and so on. Similarly, headings of the same rank should represent topics of roughly equal importance. Paradoxically, though, the less prominent the heading, the more specific and precise must be the wording below it.

Think of it this way. You are driving from London to South Wales. As you approach the motorway you see a large sign giving fairly general directions: 'Wales and the West'. As you cross the Severn Bridge you face a smaller sign providing more detailed information: 'Newport', 'Cardiff', 'Swansea'. As you leave the motorway at Newport you observe an even smaller sign giving quite detailed information: 'Retail Park', 'The Docks', 'Town Centre'. As you enter the industrial estate you see a very small sign giving details of every individual store: 'B&Q', 'Comet', 'Tesco'.

The principle applies equally to reports: the more prominent the heading, the less specific the text; the less prominent the heading, the more specific the text.

It is better to structure the report with several short sections, each containing a few subheadings, than to have just a few sections, each with several subheadings, sub-subheadings or even sub-sub-subheadings.

Numbering

The role of numbering systems is simply to identify the various components of a report for reference and indexing purposes. There are two aspects to this:

♦ numbering pages

♦ numbering sections and paragraphs.

Pages

Any time you have more than one or two pages, you need to number them. Computer software has the capability of performing this function automatically, but you must determine where you want the page numbers. Several choices are acceptable – either the upper or lower outside corners or the middle of the bottom of the page. Placing the numbers on the outside corners allows readers to locate a specific page more easily when scanning through a report.

You can number the pages by following one of two methods. Either simply number the pages from 1 to n (n representing the final page number), beginning with the page *after* the title page. Or number the 'preliminaries' (the components *before* the main body) as (i), (ii), (iii), etc – again beginning with the page *after* the title page, and number the remainder of the report from 1 to n.

Sections and paragraphs

When it comes to numbering sections and paragraphs, it is very important to keep the system simple. For many writers the numbering seems to be an end in itself; and sometimes it appears that it determines the structure rather than vice versa. Here are some possible methods:

(i) Combination of Roman and Arabic numbers

Popular throughout continental Europe, and used in all European Commission reports, Roman numerals identify sections and Arabic numerals identify related text. The breakdown is extended by decimals, if required. For example, the third section of a report could be numbered as follows:

III
    III.1
        III.1.1
        III.1.2
        III.1.3

    III.2
        III.2.1
        III.2.2

(ii) Sections with unique sequential paragraph numbers
Here Arabic numbers are used to identify sections, letters are used for subheadings and Roman numerals for sub-subheadings. For example:

> 5(a)i
> 5(a)ii
> 5(b)i
> 5(b)ii
> 5(b)iii

(iii) Simple decimal numbers
This method uses a two- or three-decimal numbering system, combined with Roman numerals to identify paragraphs within subsections or sub-subsections:

> 4.
>   4.1
>   4.1.1
>   4.1.2
>   (i)
>   (ii)
>   4.1.3

(iv) All-decimal system
However, the most popular scheme of numbering is the all-decimal system. There is no provision for any symbols other than decimal combinations. Reports numbered in this way are clear and unambiguous, but they can easily become extremely cumbersome:

> 1.1.1.1
> 1.1.1.2
> 1.2.1.1
> 1.2.1.2
> 1.2.2.1
> 1.2.2.2
> 1.2.2.3

By numbering **paragraphs** rather than headings or subheadings, you can avoid the complexity of three-part (1.1.1), four-part (1.1.1.1), or even five-part (1.1.1.1.1) numbering.

If your organisation has no standard numbering system for use in all its reports (it **should** have one), ask yourself what system would make things as easy as possible for your readers. Look at earlier reports. What numbering systems did they employ? Which of them worked best? Would it work equally well for this report? Always remember that a numbering system should be determined by the structure of the report, not vice versa.

Checklist: layout and design

♦ Keep paragraphs fairly short (generally five to eight lines) – particularly when using two- or three-column layouts.

♦ Break up text by using the technique of listing (enumerating) with bullet, checkmark, arrow, or some other interesting character.

♦ Make your page breaks so that you avoid widow or orphan lines – one line stranded from the rest of the paragraph.

♦ Avoid mixed or uneven columns, which result in a lack of visual continuity. Stick to one column grid for each page.

♦ Aim for a minimum of 30 per cent and an average 50 per cent white space on each page.

TYPOGRAPHY

Typography is the art and style of printing. Today users have at their disposal literally thousands of **typefaces** (specific type designs) and **fonts** (sets of characters in one weight and style of typeface) from which to choose. The choice of type is important because it will set the psychological mood and style of a report and create an impression of formality or informality. Be selective, and, if appropriate, consider taking advice from a designer who could help you develop a departmental or corporate identity that works for your business.

But more likely, *you* will choose the type for your report. Three elements must be considered:

♦ kinds of type

♦ size of type

♦ type alignment.

Kinds of type

Type can be classified into many different categories. One category is *serif or sans serif.* Serif is the French word for tails and it refers to the small cross strokes or flares at the end of a letter's main stems. Even though sans serif (meaning without tails) provides a cleaner, simpler look, some people believe that a serif type is more distinguished as well as easier to read.

Serif

Sans Serif

Typeface refers to a specific type design. Limit your selection to just one or two typefaces in any particular report.

Century Old Style Bold

Arial Narrow

A **type family** includes all the variations of a basic design in every weight and point size. These variations are also called typestyle and include:

Bold

Italics

Bold Italics

<u>Underline</u>

Fonts are complete sets of characters (the alphabet, numbers and symbols) in one weight and style of typeface. Here are *Gill Sans Light* (*regular*) and *Univers Condensed* (*bold*):

AaBbCcDdEeFfGgHhIiJjKkLlMmNnOoPpQq
RrSsTtUuVvWwXxYyZzO123456789!"#$%

AaBbCcDdEeFfGgHhIiJjKkLlMmNnOoPpQqRrSs
TtUuVvWwXxYyZzO123456789!"#$%&shifted()*+,

Sizes of type

Type is measured by using the language of printer-points and picas. A point (1/72 of an inch) is the smallest typographical unit of measurement. A pica is approximately 12 points or 1/6 of an inch. On a computer, text can range in size from very small to very large.

4 6 8 9 **10 12**

16 18 20

36 42

72

The usual size for report text is 10- or 12-point.

Headings are normally made in **bold** to capture the reader's attention, and can vary in size to show the level of importance. As we have already seen, the more important the heading, the larger the letters. For this reason, a hierarchy of sizes and styles is needed for showing the various levels of headings and subheadings. The plan should be consistent and logical and progress from higher to lower levels in an obvious pattern. For instance, a heading could use an 18-point, bold font. A subheading could be reduced to 14-point bold. A sub-subheading could be 12-point bold italics. If a fourth level is needed, it could be an indented paragraph heading using italicized type the size of the text.

If you recall the analogy of the car journey from London to South Wales, under this hierarchy of sizes and styles, the signposts you encounter would have looked like this:

Heading:	**Wales and the West**
Subheading:	**Newport**
Sub-subheading:	***Retail Park***
Fourth level:	*B&Q*

Sometimes it is useful to draw attention to parts of the text by methods other than headings. The major ways of doing this are by:

◆ Using upper case (capital) rather than lower case (small) letters.

◆ Changing the spacing either before or after the emphasised word(s).

◆ Indenting the words or text.

◆ Bulleting the words or text.

◆ Underlining the words or text.

◆ Double spacing the text.

◆ Using characters with different width (pitch).

◆ Using different typefaces or fonts.

With any form of emphasis, it is important to be consistent and not to overdo it. The more things you emphasise, the less powerful each emphasis becomes. Also, when highlighting text, remember that:

USING UPPER-CASE LETTERS, SPECIALLY IN ITALICS AND IN AN UNFAMILIAR TYPEFACE, MAKES SENTENCES DIFFICULT TO READ AND COMPREHEND.

Using bold lower-case letters makes life much easier for the reader.

Type alignment

Type alignment of left, centred, right or justified is possible either before or after the words are keyed into the computer. Justification, making both the left and right margins flush, gives a report a blocked look and is preferred by some report writers. However, research has shown that readability is improved if a ragged right margin is used. The uneven line endings provide a visual support for the eyes in addition to giving a more artistic look to the page. The choice is one for personal judgement (see Figure 7).

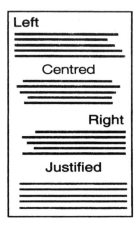

Fig. 7. Type alignment.

Checklist: typography

♦ Use no more than two different fonts in any one document – possibly a sans serif for headings and a serif for the body, or vice versa.

♦ Experiment with different typestyles – bold, italics, shadow, outline or a combination of these styles.

♦ Prefer clear typefaces that invite the readers' attention.

♦ Use italics rather than underlining the names of books or magazines.

♦ Remember to vary font size for better reading.

♦ Watch out for poor alignment. Keep everything neat and tidy.

♦ Do not cram too much in. Space creates a light, readable quality.

♦ Set up a house-style to use in your reports.

ILLUSTRATIONS

Well produced and *appropriate* illustrations really enhance a report. They make the information readily understandable, easily digestible and memorable. It is much easier to assimilate information presented pictorially. Anything on a page other than text is either artwork or graphics. The word **artwork** refers to the *images* in the report, such as photographs, drawings and cartoons; **graphics** are *image enhancements*, such as lines, boxes and background tints.

When to use illustrations

Illustrations are useful only when they are easier to understand than the words or figures they represent. Artwork and graphics should clarify, add to, illustrate, or enhance the document in some way. They should not be used without a specific reason or purpose. Otherwise, they will merely distract and confuse your readers. Ask yourself the 'so what?' question: does every illustration have something to say within the overall context of the report? If there is no meaningful answer to 'so what?', then the illustration is worthless. If you have a positive answer to the question, then the illustration *should* be included.

Where to use visual illustrations

The algorithm on page 20 will help you decide where the illustration should be placed. Ask yourself whether it would break the flow of the report or distract the reader. If the answer is 'no', place it in the main body of the report, after, and as close as possible to the point of reference. If the answer is 'yes', put it in an appendix.

Another good way to help you decide the placing of an illustration is to ask yourself whether it is **fundamental** to the arguments in the text, or **supplementary** to them. If the reader *needs* to see an illustration in order to understand the text – or if it is referred to several times – it should be placed within the main body of the report. If the reader does not need to see it, it may be preferable to place it in an appendix, particularly if there are several other illustrations.

How to use illustrations

Artwork can be inserted in your report in two ways – by using either the **traditional pasteup** method or the electronic pasteup method. In the traditional pasteup method, you simply leave space for the art. Before reproducing the copy on a duplicating machine, you paste the artwork in place. In an **electronic pasteup**, you will have the entire document on disk and can make a copy or copies from the printer.

Computer images come in two types, **vector** and **bitmap**. Vector images are created from lines and shapes, each being mathematically described within the software. The advantage with vector images is that they can be manipulated by element and easily resized. Bitmap images describe a colour photograph type of image, when stored on a computer. While it is not possible to manipulate an element of an image as you can with vector, clever software offers smart tools which allow areas of a picture to be selected and transformed and smart filters, provided with the software, make it simple to experiment with hundreds of special effects.

Electronic art can come from a variety of sources and can be imported into your document from:

♦ Drawings or diagrams created on the computer from a draw or paint program such as *CoralDRAW*, *Illustrator*, *FreeHand* or *MacDraw*.

♦ Artwork created by someone else and sold as clip art that you can copy and paste into your document.

♦ Drawings or photographs scanned into the computer using a special scanner – such work may need to be modified or retouched using a computer program such as *Adobe Photoshop*, Corel's *PaintShop Pro* or Macromedia's *Fireworks*.

♦ Graphs or charts created from a spreadsheet program such as *Excel* or *Quatro Pro*. If you wanted a pie chart showing which product ranges make up which part of your business, or a bar chart showing turnover each month of the year, then a spreadsheet would allow you to produce these.

♦ Standard camera film can be developed and printed in the normal way, but also written onto a CD-Rom in the form of high-resolution scans that can read straight into an image manipulation package on a PC. For an additional charge, *Kodak Photo CD* will provide this service.

♦ Digital cameras, used in conjunction with their own software, enable easy storage of and access to your images. Most medium to high-end cameras will offer you a choice of file formats in which to save your images. The most popular ones are JPEG, TIFF and RAW. As far as quality and versatility goes, RAW files are the best. However, RAW files also take the most work to get great-looking images.

♦ Not all digital cameras will offer TIFF as a choice, but when you have both TIFF and JPEG available, consider the following facts. TIFF files are higher quality than JPEGs yet they are also much larger. This will cause your camera to slow down when trying to write your images to the memory card loaded into your computer. That also means that the number of images you can capture in a minute will be much less with TIFF than with JPEG.

♦ Most professionals will choose JPEG when they either want to fit a large number of images on a storage card, when they are capturing fast action or when they do not want to spend time in *Photoshop* adjusting their images. However, if they want the highest quality possible, and do not mind spending some time adjusting their images, they will choose RAW.

◆ Video can be captured as stills with a video capture card. However, the quality is inferior to that of digital or scanned photographs.

Once an image is captured, the effects you can apply are almost limitless; or they can be re-sized, edited, combined and retouched at will, before they are used in reports created by your word processing or desktop publishing package.

The choice of illustrations

Your aim is to include artwork which arouses readers' interest and helps them to a quicker and fuller understanding. Do not try to be clever. Use clear, simple, uncluttered and appropriate illustrations, concentrating on the essentials.

By also including some graphics – lines, boxes, patterns and background tints – you can make your report even more stimulating and appealing to readers. Uninterrupted blocks of text are daunting. Lines, arrows, boxes, frames and shading are useful in creating divisions (see Figure 8). Icons or symbols available in various fonts will help focus or direct the readers' attention. Logos provide a subtle way of marketing your company or providing a theme for a product or topic.

Ask yourself: What is the **purpose** of the illustration? Let us consider three of the most common answers to this question:

◆ To give a general impression.

◆ To show detailed information.

◆ To show the structure and working of a system.

Illustrations which give a general impression

Three of the best ways of illustrating this are by the use of a:

♦ pie chart

♦ bar chart

♦ pictogram.

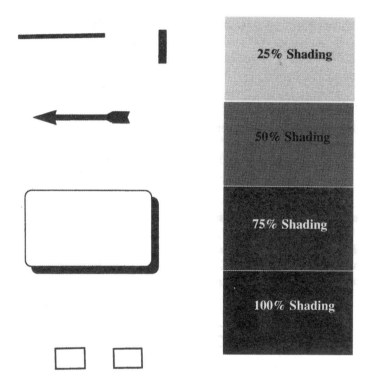

Fig. 8.   Lines, arrows, boxes, frames and shading.

Pie charts

A pie chart is a circle divided by radii into sectors whose areas are proportional to the relative magnitudes of a set of items. It is an excellent method of illustrating such **relative proportions**.

Here is an example. In 2010, total advertising expenditure in the UK was as follows:

Press	:	£8,303 million
Television	:	£4,579 million
Direct mail	:	£2,318 million
Internet	:	£2,016 million
Outdoor	:	£1,083 million
Radio	:	£532 million
Cinema	:	£190 million

Computer software will do all the calculations for you, but if you need to work out the number of degrees in each sector yourself, use this equation:

$$\frac{\text{Sector total x } 360°}{\text{Total population}}$$

For example, the calculation for the press is:

$$\frac{8303 \times 360°}{19021} = 157°$$

Three variations on the basic pie chart are the:

♦ illustrated pie chart

♦ half-pie chart

♦ multi-pie chart.

The **illustrated pie chart** simply includes some illustration or drawing relevant to each slice of the pie. In the example given in Figure 9, it probably would be a few newspapers, a television set, and so on.

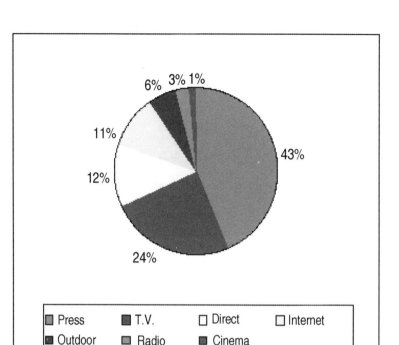

Fig. 9.   A pie chart.

The **half-pie chart** depicts only the top half of a circle. To calculate the number of degrees appropriate to each division, multiply by 180° instead of 360°.

The **multi-pie chart** consists of two or more pie charts each with similar component parts. The size of each pie chart will depend on its relative importance. For example, a pie chart illustrating the distribution of trade in the USA would be larger than one for Britain. These charts are quite difficult to draw.

Bar charts
This is a simple way of comparing values by using bars of various lengths, drawn to scale. In other words, it is an excellent way of illustrating **relationships** between items. Figure 10 is a bar chart showing the main crops grown in Britain during 2010.

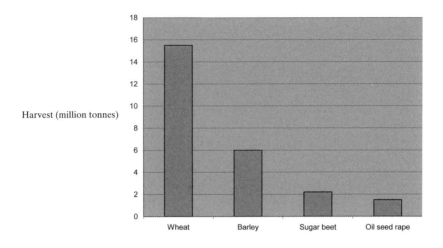

Fig. 10.   A bar chart.

Variations on the basic bar chart include the:

♦   Sectional bar chart

♦   Percentage bar chart

♦   Dual bar chart.

Sectional bar charts show the magnitude of items *and* their constituent parts. For example, a chart showing passenger traffic at Britain's four main airports in 2000, 2005 and 2010 would comprise three bars (showing the total traffic for the three years), each divided into four (showing the traffic going through the individual airports).

Percentage bar charts show the percentage a constituent part bears to the whole. For example, if you wanted to compare the number of votes cast for political parties at the last general election with the number of candidates elected, you would show two bars of identical size; one divided to reflect the percentage of total votes cast for each party, the other the percentage of total MPs elected.

Dual bar charts compare two or more related quantities over time. For example, they could show the percentage of households with cars, central heating and telephones in 2000 and 2010. For each of these there would be two bar charts, next to each other, one for 2000 and one for 2010.

Pictogram
This is similar to a bar chart except that it is usually horizontal and it uses symbols instead of bars to represent magnitudes or frequencies. Figure 11 is a pictogram which shows the passenger traffic at Britain's main airports in 2010.

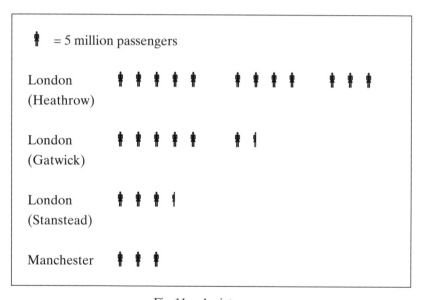

Fig. 11. A pictogram.

Illustrations which show detailed information

These illustrations must facilitate detailed readings or provide detailed answers to questions. Three of the most effective ways of achieving these aims are by the use of:

- graph

- algorithm

- table.

Graph

A graph shows the relationship between two variables, and it is an excellent method of illustrating detailed relationships between items. The **vertical axis** is usually scaled in units of the dependent variable (the quantity which is being controlled or adjusted), while the **horizontal axis** is usually scaled in units of the independent variable (the quantity being observed).

A variation on the **simple graph** is the pictorial line graph where 'pictures' are added. For example, if you were comparing the efficiency of postal services in different parts of the world, you could superimpose national stamps to distinguish the countries represented by the various lines on the graph. However, be careful not to make any graph too complex. There are also several other types of graph, each associated with one or more professions. For example, a financial or management accountant would be interested in break-even charts, investment risk profiles, sensitivity analyses, and so on.

Here are some rules to follow when drawing graphs:

- When undertaking experimental work, draw a rough graph as you record your results. In this way you can check any irregularities immediately.

- Choose a scale in which the lines or the curve will occupy most of the graph.

- If possible the graph should be arranged so that it reads the same way up as the text.

♦ In most experimental work, lines should form smooth curves.

♦ Where results do not follow a smooth curve, or where the graph does not represent experimental findings (perhaps it shows sales results), points should be joined by straight lines. Where this occurs you *cannot* read off between the points as with a curve.

Algorithm

An algorithm is a flow chart which will answer a question, or solve a problem, or undertake a procedure, within a finite number of steps. It does this by considering only those factors that are relevant to the question, problem or procedure. Algorithms are often difficult to write but, once prepared, they are excellent illustrations, particularly for instructional manuals. For example, they can be used to describe fault finding procedures, or how to carry out complicated checks on machinery. They can be used by readers with no knowledge of operational theory. In Chapter 1 (Figure 2), there is a very simple algorithm to help the report writer decide whether to include a particular piece of information in the report and, if so, where to place it.

Table

Your aim is to make the report as readable as possible and the use of a table is often the best way of achieving this aim while also presenting some essential, detailed information.

A common mistake in writing reports is to produce too many figures and too few explanations. The principles to follow are three-fold:

♦ Always check figures very carefully before including them.

♦ Restrict figures to those which are meaningful.

♦ Make sure they are consistently produced and interpreted.

However, in some reports it is essential to include a large number of highly detailed findings. The strength of these reports is often based almost entirely on their factual content. In such cases it is usually best to use **appendixes.** Where appropriate, it is perfectly acceptable for your appendixes to be longer than all the rest of the report. But think of your readers. How are they likely to read the report? They will probably read the preliminaries and then the main body. The appendixes may well be an afterthought. So highlight any particularly significant findings in these preliminaries and in the main body. If you find it necessary to refer to certain tables on several occasions, it is better to include them in the main body.

Here are some rules when compiling statistical tables:

♦   Avoid tables where there are over ten columns.

♦   Label each column and row to identify the data.

♦   If a column shows amounts, state the units.

♦   If columns are too long, double space after every fifth entry.

♦   If a particular column or row lacks data, use dashes in each space lacking the data.

♦   If they improve legibility, use vertical lines to separate columns.

♦   Do not mix decimals (29.3) with fractions (17½).

Never assume that your readers will draw the right conclusion from the figures. They may quite easily not be reading them at all; or they may read them and come to the wrong conclusions, or perhaps no conclusions. Always say in words what they mean.

Illustrations which show the structure and working of a system

Here the word 'system' is used in its widest sense to include any structure or process composed of interrelated, interdependent, or interacting elements forming a collective entity. The management structure of a company is a system. So is a clerical or production process. So is the way a piece of machinery is built, and is used.

Three of the best ways of illustrating the structure and working of a system are by the use of a:

♦ chart

♦ diagram

♦ photograph.

Chart
We have already considered pie charts, bar charts and graphs. Other charts of potential value to report writers include:

♦ flow charts

♦ organisational charts

♦ maps and plans

♦ systematic diagrams.

A **flow chart** is a diagrammatic representation of the sequence of operations or equipment in a natural, industrial or organisational process. It is commonly used to describe industrial and clerical processes, and computer systems and programs. Figure 12 is a flow chart illustrating inventory control by means of the calculation of the value of the inventory. As you will see, a flow chart uses a standard set of symbols. In this instance the symbols are those associated with computer science.

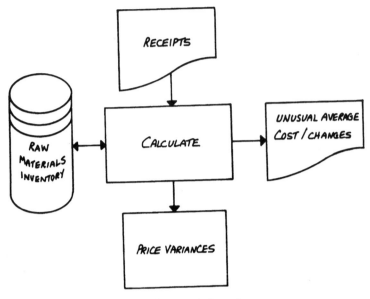

Fig. 12.   A flow chart.

An organisational chart depicts the hierarchy of, and the lines of command, within an organisation. Figure 13 represents a simple organisation which could well exist within the transport services function of a small manufacturing company.

When **maps** or **plans** are included in a report it is important to state whether or not they are completely to scale. Always include a small arrow pointing northwards.

Systematic diagrams are useful when you wish to illustrate what connects with what. They are commonly used for wiring diagrams and transport connections. The famous map of the London Underground is an example of a systematic diagram.

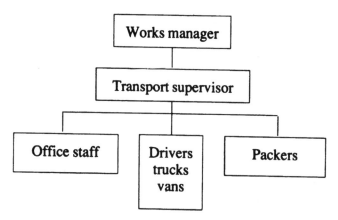

Fig. 13.   An organisational chart.

Diagram

This is a drawing or sketch which demonstrates the form or working of something. There are several types of diagram, including:

♦   orthographic drawing

♦   isometric drawing

♦   perspective drawing

♦   exploded drawing

♦   cut-away drawing.

An **orthographic drawing** is composed of the plans of the back, front and side elevations of an object. It must be drawn to scale. While it is very useful for designers and manufacturers, it is of little value for anyone who wants to know what it actually looks like.

An **isometric drawing** provides a pictorial method of illustrating something. Three faces are shown at once but no allowance is made for perspective; all the lines that are parallel on the object are drawn parallel. It is easy to draw but the lack of perspective makes it look peculiar, as can be seen in Figure 14.

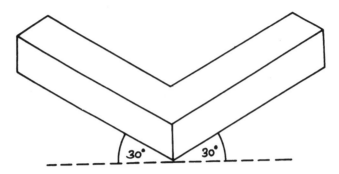

Fig. 14.   An isometric drawing.

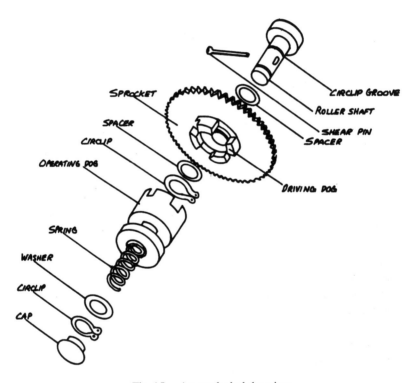

Fig. 15.   An exploded drawing.

A **perspective drawing**, on the other hand, shows an object as it is seen by the human eye. It is more difficult to draw but it looks more natural.

An **exploded drawing** provides a pictorial representation of how something is constructed. It does this by showing its components in assembly as though they were spread out along an invisible axis. Figure 15 is an exploded drawing of a lawn mower dog clutch.

A **cut-away drawing** shows an object with its 'cover off' in certain places, or with a slice removed to reveal the inside. Figure 16 is a cut-away drawing of an electric bell.

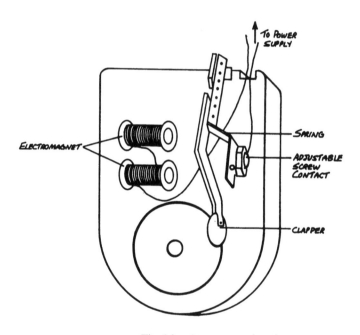

Fig. 16. A cut-away drawing.

In general, a line drawing is better for technical illustrations than a photograph since it can be shaded or highlighted to emphasise essential points. It also reproduces well. However, a report writer should also consider whether the inclusion of a photograph would be useful and justifiable.

Photograph

A *good* photograph will show the exact appearance of an object or a situation at a particular moment in time. It is therefore useful for showing newly created objects, ones never seen before, ones at the end of a particular stage of development, or ones worn out or damaged. If you need to show the size of an object, it is a good idea to include some familiar object in the photograph – perhaps a hand, a finger, a coin, or a ruler.

Unless you are already a very competent photographer, it is best to keep things as simple as possible. Use an automatic 35mm SLR (Single Lens Reflex) or a digital camera. You will see exactly what has been captured; you will achieve an accurate focus; you will be using a system of lenses and accessories which will allow an enormous variety and flexibility of output, and you can expect good results in a variety of lighting conditions.

However, **things do go wrong** – especially if you are not an experienced photographer. For this reason also use a back up Polaroid camera. You will be able to see your results within seconds. If you are not satisfied with them, keep clicking away until you are.

Checklist: visual illustrations

♦ Use artwork to enhance, illustrate or provide additional information.

♦ Make sure it proves what you intended it to prove.

♦ Refer to it in the text *before* it appears, not after.

♦ Discuss and explain its significance.

♦ Size art to fit your needs but be sure that you keep it in proportion.

♦ Use a sensible scale and give details of this scale.

- Crop art to eliminate unwanted portions.

- Keep it simple; do not include too much detail.

- Do not use so many special effects that they cease to be special.

- Do not overdo it; too many illustrations will overwhelm the reader. One large image is far more eye-catching than half a dozen small ones.

- Make sure that any artwork (including charts and graphs) is viewed at the same distance as the text – a reader should not have to hold a page closer or farther away when looking at an illustration.

- Give each illustration a caption and figure number.

- Where appropriate, acknowledge your source.

- If there are more than just one or two illustrations, list them on the contents page.

- Remember that non-digitized art can be mechanically pasted up and reproduced on a copying machine or taken to a professional printer.

COLOUR

Colour adds a whole new look to a document. Today, full-colour computer-generated reports can be a reality through **ink jet, thermal** or **laser printing**. Systems are becoming more sophisticated all the time and as the technology is advancing, so the price of having colour printers connected to your computer is decreasing. Black and white reports have become as outdated as black and white television sets.

Another option worth considering is the use of coloured paper. Light-tinted paper with black type is less glaring for readers. In addition, the use of a variety of colours of paper is helpful in coding your work. For instance, different sections can be produced in different colours or a variety of handouts can be made in a variety of colours for easier referencing.

Coloured paper:

♦ prevents glare

♦ codes pages

♦ adds variety.

Several companies now provide paper with pre-printed colour designs. Many also offer computer templates which enable you to see these designs onscreen. Print, graphics and art can then be planned and keyed aesthetically around them. When you insert the paper into the tray of the printer, you are able to run black print onto the design. The result is the look of a full-colour document.

In general, for most documents you will want to use a light background with dark type (see Figure 17). Full-colour clip art is available for importing into your documents. A revolution is now underway in using colour for presentations, and the use of colour for reports will become more and more available in the future.

Sophisticated readers of today expect and deserve more than black printing on a white background. Use this to your advantage. Colour creates moods, sensations and impressions that can be highly effective in achieving your objectives.

Checklist: colour

♦ Be sure that you have the capability to print in colour at an affordable price before planning and producing your report in colour.

- Limit the use of colour to about three or four pages unless full colour is used.

- Use sufficient contrast for effective reading – dark print on light background or light print on dark background.

- Give objects their proper colour, such as green leaves or yellow bananas.

- Remember that approximately ten per cent of males and seven per cent of females are colour-blind – red and green used side by side may merge.

Fig. 17.   Contrasting backgrounds and type.

PAPER, COVERS, BINDING AND INDEXING

Finally, a word about the choice of paper, covers, binding and possible indexing for your report. Appearance really does matter. So does durability. It is obvious that glossy, professional-looking reports will project the sort of image that most companies wish to foster with existing and potential customers and/or shareholders. Perhaps what is less obvious is that sometimes it is desirable to produce low-budget reports for more than just reasons of economy. For example, it is rarely necessary to produce an ornate product if it is for internal consumption only. Even if your department does have money to burn, it is not a good idea to advertise the fact.

As you think about the physical construction and appearance of a report, bear these points in mind:

♦ Your purpose (the **action** you intend the report to generate).

♦ The readership (number and nature).

♦ The expected life of the report (including the number of likely references to be made to it).

♦ What materials and facilities are available within your organisation.

♦ The cost of these various options (and your budget).

Paper

There are three aspects to consider when choosing paper, namely its:

♦ size

♦ quality

♦ colour.

Most reports are written on **A4 size paper** (210 x 297 mm). However, there are other possibilities (see page 113). The **quality of paper** you choose will depend on all the factors listed above. For example, do not use poor quality paper if the report is likely to be referred to frequently.

The importance of **conciseness** has been stressed throughout this book. However, this does not mean use as little paper as possible. It is also important not to present the reader with huge blocks of uninterrupted type. If you are really concerned about the future of the Scandinavian and Amazonian forests, the amount of paper saved at the planning stage will more than compensate for an extra few sheets in the report itself.

It is customary for reports to be written on white paper. However, as we have seen, sometimes it is useful to use different **colour paper** in different sections of the report. If you do this be sure that:

◆ The colours are easily distinguishable.

◆ Dark colours are avoided.

◆ The different sections are logical and rational.

Alternatively, you could use white paper throughout and coloured partitions between the sections.

Covers

Every report should have covers, if only an extra sheet of paper at the back and front to serve as a dust jacket. However, most reports will be enclosed by glossy boards (cards). Other covers will be made of plastic or even imitation leather, perhaps with a pocket so that other related documents can be kept with the report. Customised covers on a report can set it apart.

Covers protect reports which are likely to be read by many people or saved for a long period of time. A report is twice as likely to be read and three times as likely to be saved if it has attractive (though not necessarily expensive) covers.

Many reports will have no more than a title on their covers. Others will include the organisation's name and logo and/or a space for a reference number, the date of issue and the name of the department responsible for the production of the report. Sometimes a 'window' will have been cut out of the front cover. This allows the reader to see the title as it appears on the title page.

Think carefully about the colour of your covers. Dark ones are often very depressing while very light ones or ones using a combination of bright colours may give an unwanted impression of light-heartedness. 'Safe' colours for reports are either blue or green.

Binding

There are several inexpensive binding systems available. Your choice will depend largely upon:

♦ The size of the report.

♦ Whether amendments will be necessary.

♦ Whether inserts will be necessary.

♦ The distribution requirements.

♦ The quality requirements.

♦ The binding methods used for other related reports.

♦ What system or systems are available within your organisation.

Here are some common methods of binding:

♦ treasury tag

♦ stapling

♦ plastic gripper

♦ gluing

♦ stitching

♦ ring binding.

Treasury tag

Tags come in various sizes identified by their colour. Punch a hole in the top left of the report. Make sure it is at least an inch into the paper both from the top and the left, otherwise sheets will soon become detached. For larger reports, also punch a hole at the bottom left, or use a four-hole punch. This method of binding is suitable where amendments will be likely and/or where inserts such as maps and plans are expected. Do not use tags to bind reports which are larger than 100 sheets.

Stapling

Here you simply staple the covers and pages at the top left corner. For reports of 10 to 20 pages, it is best to staple them from the front and the back. Then place the report in a plastic wallet. A more sophisticated method is to staple down the left hand side and cover them with adhesive binding strip. Be sure to leave wide margins, and double staple at the top and bottom of the report. Never use paper clips. Pins are slightly better, but for reasons of safety they are not recommended.

Plastic gripper

This method is an improvement on the use of staples down the left side of the report, but the principle is the same. Use a plastic slide-grip along the left hand edge of the assembled covers and sheets. Once again, remember to leave wide margins if you intend to use this system.

Gluing

The edges of the sheets are glued and fixed into the spine of a fabric, card or plastic cover. This method is suitable only for reports of about 25 pages or more and it should be attempted only by the most dexterous of report writers. A more sophisticated method is known as hot metal gluing.

Stitching

Here the report is made up of sheets folded in the middle to make two single-sided or four double-sided pages. They are then bound by a method known as saddle stitching. This system is not suitable for larger reports because the pages tend to become distorted. It is possible to have reports stitched and cased commercially in hardback form. However, this would be a far more expensive exercise.

Ring binding

This gives a report a professional appearance and it is suitable for works of up to around 20 sheets. You will need to have access to a special machine which perforates the binding edge and then threads the binding (plastic or wire) through the holes in the covers and the report. The pages of the report will then lie flat when opened. Plastic binding is preferred because sheets can be added or removed, as required. This is not possible with wire binding. Any organisation which produces reports regularly and/or in quantity should seriously consider acquiring a ring binding machine.

Indexing

The report will have a contents page and it may have an index. It is possible to improve the presentation further by making it even easier for readers to find their way around the report. This can be done in a number of ways, as illustrated in Figure 18.

The thumb-index pages method is quite complex and it needs to be undertaken professionally. Therefore it is only appropriate where there will be a wide external circulation. On the other hand, the overlapping pages method is very simple: each section is identified by pages of unique width. It is most suitable for short reports. Side indexing is another straightforward method. It is achieved simply by attaching protruding self-adhesive labels to the first page of each section of the report. Each of these methods can be complemented by the use of different colour pages to identify the various sections of the report.

Thumb-index pages

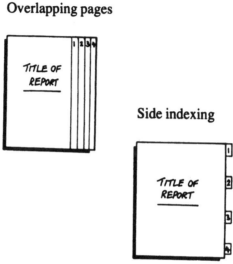

Fig. 18. Indexing a report.

SUMMARY

Appearance matters. The way you present your text and artwork, and your choice of paper, covers, binding and possibly indexing, will be strongly influenced by your purpose, your readership, the expected life of the report, the options available to you within your organisation, and their relative cost.

Word processing and desktop publishing

Modern word processing and desktop publishing packages present opportunities to the report writer that were unthinkable a decade ago. However, do not get carried away with the possibilities. Remember that your purpose is to communicate *simply* and *effectively* with your readers.

Layout and design

Presentation can be greatly assisted if sufficient thought is given to the report's:

♦ format

♦ page size and orientation

♦ margins and spacing

♦ headings and subheadings

♦ numbering.

Typography

This is the art and style of printing. A very wide range of typefaces and fonts is available. Be selective, and choose ones that will help you develop the right departmental or corporate image and identity for your business.

Illustrations

♦ Well produced and *appropriate* illustrations really enhance a report. They make information readily understandable, easily digestible and memorable. It is easier to assimilate information presented pictorially.

♦ However, illustrations should only be used if they are easier to understand than the words or figures they represent. They should *never* be included for their own sake. Ask yourself: are they relevant to the text?

♦ Before you decide the kind of illustration you will use, ask yourself what is its *purpose:* is it intended to give an overall impression of something, to show some detailed findings, or to show the structure and working of a system? Then choose the most appropriate illustration to achieve this end.

♦ If a reader will *need* to see the illustration in order to understand the text, place it as close to the point of reference as possible. However, if it is merely *supplementary* to the text, it is often preferable to place it in an appendix.

Colour

Reports printed only in black, and always against a white background, have become as old fashioned as black and white television sets. Today's technology can make full colour printing a reality.

Paper, covers, binding and indexing

Finally, consider the overall appearance and required durability of your report.

♦ Think about the size, quality and colour of paper you will require.

♦ Remember that your report should have covers and that customised ones would set it apart.

♦ Consider which binding system you will use.

♦ Ask yourself whether the report should be indexed and, if so, which would be the best method to employ.

Part Three

Some Common Types of Report

- ◆ Accident reports
- ◆ Agendas for committee meetings
- ◆ Annual reports
- ◆ Appraisal reports
- ◆ Audit reports
- ◆ Comparative testing reports
- ◆ Duty notes reports
- ◆ Explanatory reports
- ◆ Feasibility reports
- ◆ Informative reports
- ◆ Instructional manuals

- Interview reports

- Investigation into financial affairs of a company reports

- Minutes

- Process description reports

- Progress reports

- Research reports

- Scientific reports

- Student project reports

- Systems evaluation reports

- Technical reports

- Technological reports

- Trouble-shooting reports.

This section considers some of the most common types of report which you may be required to produce. They cover different subjects, and have different purposes and readerships. For this reason they have different structures; they are made up of a variety of combinations of report components (introductions, summaries, and so on), and these components are often given different names in different types of report. Every report should have a title page.

In Chapter 1 we discussed report components in some detail. The comments here are intended to complement that discussion by pointing out the **particular emphases** associated with each report type. We shall do this by answering two questions:

1. What points should I bear in mind?

2. What would be a suitable format?

Use this information and advice to help you decide the most appropriate style, format and contents for your report. However, use them **flexibly**; you must also bear in mind:

♦ The requirements of the person who commissioned the report.

♦ House-style.

♦ Custom and conventions.

♦ Your objective(s).

♦ Your readership.

♦ Common sense.

As you plan and later draft your report, remember that while every report should be different, every report also should have some similarities. It must present relevant facts accurately and in a way that is both acceptable and intelligible to its readers. In other words, it must have a beginning, a middle and an end. Only then can you expect to achieve these three essential aims:

♦ to be read without unnecessary delay

♦ to be understood without undue effort

♦ and to be accepted.

So always think about the needs of your readers. They are the important people, and they have a right to expect you to make things as easy for them as possible. If you do not help them, why should they help you? Refer also to Appendix 2 to see how the style, layout and content of a report should reflect its overall purpose and readership.

ACCIDENT REPORTS

These reports hopefully will not be required on a regular basis.

What points should I bear in mind?

Balance speed with accuracy. The reason for speed is so that all salient facts are accurately recorded before details are forgotten. The reasons for accuracy are to minimise the risk of any possible recurrence, to comply with the law and to be prepared to face a possible claim for damages. You will require accurate illustrations supplemented by statements from participants, witnesses and experts.

What would be a suitable format?

If you have no formal report form, use these headings:

1.   What was the accident?

2.   Where and when did it occur?

3.   Who was involved?

4.   Was any injury sustained? If so, what was it?

5.   Who reported the accident?

6.   What medical treatment was applied – when and by whom?

7.   What caused the accident?

8.   What has been done to correct the trouble?

9.   What recommendations do you have to avoid a recurrence?

AGENDAS FOR COMMITTEE MEETINGS

An agenda is a list of items to be discussed during a meeting. It *must* be drawn up in advance.

What points should I bear in mind?

An agenda may take various forms, according to the requirements and, in some cases, the kind of meeting to which it refers. Be sure you know precisely what is expected of you. Here are two common forms of committee agenda:

♦ the standard agenda

♦ the discussive agenda.

The standard agenda simply lists the subjects to be discussed, and the order in which they will be taken.

The discussive agenda is designed to stimulate thought *before* and comment *at* the meeting. It is often used for 'one-off' meetings.

No business should be placed on an agenda unless it comes within the scope of the committee, and it is within the power of the committee to deal with it. Conversely, no relevant item of business should be omitted.

In deciding what to include on an agenda, bear these points in mind:

♦ Talk to the chairperson and other committee members who may have business to include.

♦ Refer to the minutes of previous meetings for any business or discussions which were then deferred, and for reminders of routine annual, half-yearly, quarterly or monthly recurring items.

♦ Keep a special file of documents which are likely to be required at the next meeting. Sort and arrange them before drafting the agenda.

Then think carefully about the order in which items should come up for discussion. Consider these factors when deciding the order:

♦ Refer to any rules governing the meeting which regulate the order in which items of business are dealt with.

♦ If there are no such rules, make sure the items are in a logical order. Wherever possible, the end of the discussion on one item should lead naturally on to the next.

♦ It is normally preferable to put routine business first.

♦ Try to place difficult or contentious items just after half-way through the agenda, with some simple, uncontentious items before and after them. This is known as a bell-curve structure. Begin with some items likely to achieve a consensus. Then move on to your more 'difficult' subjects. Conclude with more simple, uncontentious items so that the meeting will end amicably.

Make it easy for the committee members to find their way through the agenda by using these devices:

♦ Number all items consecutively, beginning with '1'.

♦ If separate documents are required for any item, quote the reference number under the appropriate heading together with the date of circulation. If they are to be circulated later, or handed out at the meeting, say so.

♦ Where an item on the agenda is being continued or carried forward from a previous meeting, quote the minute and date of that meeting.

♦ At the end of the agenda provide a checklist of the documents required for the meeting, in the order in which they will be needed.

Finally, obtain the chairperson's approval of the agenda *before* circulating it. This agenda will form the basis of the minutes of the meeting (see below).

What would be a suitable format?

Standard agenda

A suitable format for a standard agenda would be as follows:

1. Heading (including where and when the meeting will take place)

2. Apologies for Absence

3. Minutes of the Previous Meeting

4.

5. } Items requiring the attention of the committee

6.

7.

8. Any Other Business ('leftovers', not items that should have been discussed within section 4–7)

9. Date of Next Meeting (also give the time and location)

10. Papers Required for the Meeting (in the order that they will be needed).

Items 1–3 and 8–10 are standard. Between them come all other items requiring the attention of the committee.

Discussive agenda

A discussive agenda could be structured as follows:

1. Heading (including where and when the meeting will take place)

2. Introduction (what will be discussed, and why – keep it fairly general)

3. Scope (what are the boundaries of the discussion?)

4. Discussion points (list the items to be discussed and the reasons for discussing them)

5. Possible action (what options are open to the committee?)

6. Summary (the reason for the meeting; what it hopes to achieve and why members should attend and contribute)

7. Papers required for the meeting (in the order that they will be needed).

ANNUAL REPORTS

An annual report lists the achievements and failures of an organisation. It is a progress report in which every department is accounted for.

What points should I bear in mind?

The physical appearance of annual reports is crucial. For that reason they are usually prepared professionally. The cover and the first few pages must attract and then maintain the readers' interest. Make the cover attractive and eye-catching; keep the text well spaced and content not too heavy. Begin with some simple facts about the organisation and what it does. Use short paragraphs with bold print to emphasise the key points. Include illustrations to attract interest and to break up overbearing columns of figures. When you use photographs of people, record their names. Too many reports give the name of their chairperson but then describe a member of staff as 'an engineer', or whatever. Workers, like chairpersons, have names.

As a general rule, the shorter the report the better the chances of attracting a fringe readership. So make sure you gather *relevant* data from all parts of your organisation. Obviously every department will wish to emphasise its successes and gloss over (or simply ignore) its failures. For this reason the use of standard questionnaires is recommended. This will provide only the information you require, and it will be in a uniform format and style. Use this as the basis of the main body of the report.

Annual reports usually include a chairperson's statement. Most of these statements are far too long. Tactfully explain that all that is required is a résumé and critical analysis of the past year's work, and an assessment of prospects. This section should pass logically from topic to topic. It should be informative, businesslike and balanced. It should also be concise – no more than 1,000 words (less if possible).

What would be a suitable format?
This depends on the nature of the organisation and the readership. Here is one possible format:

♦ contents list

♦ what the organisation does

♦ some of the year's highlights

♦ chairperson's statement

♦ main body (possibly department to department, or task to task)

♦ accounts

♦ appendices.

A standard format is useful for year-to-year comparisons.

APPRAISAL REPORTS

These appraise a person's performance in his or her current job, identify methods of improving this performance, highlight training needs, and often assess suitability for another job, promotion, and/or a change in salary.

What points should I bear in mind?

Appraisal reports are very important because what you write will have a direct effect on people's career prospects. They are very difficult to write. The dilemma is that, on the one hand, you need to know a person quite well in order to write a fair report while, on the other hand, it can be difficult to be objective when you know a person quite well. Not only that, you will need to decide what is relevant and what is not. For example behavioural patterns are likely to change according to circumstances, and we tend to remember extremes of behaviour. Ask yourself: 'Are they really typical?' Try keeping a notebook and update it regularly in order to build up an accurate and balanced picture of people. Also talk with them about this throughout the year, not just at counselling and appraisal interviews.

The responsibilities of an appraisal report writer, therefore, are acute. Be specific and avoid euphemisms. You must be able to justify every tick in the matrix boxes, and every word and phrase you use.

What would be a suitable format?

You may be required to complete a standard form. Details will vary from organisation to organisation, but the broad outline of an appraisal report should cover the following headings and questions:

1. The Job

♦ The job description, its objectives, component tasks, methods and resources.

- Are they satisfactory?

- If not, why not?

- What changes are required?

- What action is recommended – by whom, how and why?

2. Job Performance

- What objectives must be met and what tasks must be fulfilled?

- Have these been achieved?

- What is the actual evidence from work performance, indicating success or failure?

- How far have any failures been within or outside the job-holder's control?

- What does the evidence of past performance show about the strengths and weaknesses in knowledge, skills and attitudes of the job-holder?

- What precise action is recommended – by whom, how and when – to build on strengths, to remedy weaknesses and to develop the individual by means of training and further work experience?

3. Summary of Action Proposed

- What action has been agreed to be taken by whom, how and when?

AUDIT REPORTS

There are two types of auditor: the external auditor and the internal auditor. The role of the former is laid down by statute and in case law; that of the latter, while also affected to some extent by case law, is ultimately what management wants it to be. Therefore the structure of audit reports will depend on the type of audit work being undertaken.

External auditors are independent of the companies on which they report. They are required to report to the shareholders at general meetings on whether the final statements of a company give a 'true and fair view' of the state of the company's affairs. If they are uncertain, or if they do not believe this to be so, they must say so in what is known as a **qualified audit report**. It is now normal practice also for external auditors to issue **reports to management** which are more akin to internal audit reports.

Internal auditors are concerned with the segregation of duties and the internal control of the business for which they are employed. The structure of their reports tends to be fairly consistent, but it is *not* defined by any Auditing Standards.

What points should I bear in mind?

In a few words the external auditor commits himself or herself to a high degree of responsibility. If the contents of the report do not reflect the due care, skill and diligence expected of a qualified person, the auditor may be held liable for damages. It is essential, therefore, that the report should be carefully prepared to reflect an opinion within the limits of the examination, and sufficiently clear as to leave no likelihood of misinterpretation by those whom it concerns.

The internal auditor does not face such an onerous responsibility because the report is not written for the same audience – it is for internal consumption (although the external auditor may decide to place some reliance upon it). However, like all report writers, the internal auditor must always strive for objectivity and accuracy.

What would be a suitable format?

The usual format for an external audit report on the financial statements of a company incorporated in Great Britain is as follows:

1. Introduction

2. Respective responsibilities of directors and auditors

3. Basis of opinion

4. Opinion.

An external auditor's report to management will include any or all of the following sections:

1. Weaknesses in internal control and recommendations on how they may be rectified.

2. Breakdowns in the accounting systems and any material errors arising.

3. Additional audit time required as a result of either section 1 or 2, or the client's failure to adhere to timetables.

4. Unsatisfactory accounting procedures or policies, and recommendations as to how they may be improved.

5. Suggestions as to how financial and accounting efficiency may be improved.

6. Constructive suggestions not necessarily related to accounting procedures but noted by the auditor during the course of his or her investigations, with the benefit of an outsider's viewpoint.

A suitable format for an internal audit report is as follows:

1. Contents page

2. Summary (the main findings, conclusions and recommendations)

3. Introduction (what broad subjects were audited, where and when)

4. Scope (what precisely was audited, and possibly what was not)

5. Main body (the findings, divided into logical sub-sections)

6. Conclusions (flowing naturally from the main body)

7. Recommendations (flowing naturally from the conclusions)

8. Appendices.

COMPARATIVE TESTING REPORTS

Perhaps the best known of these reports is *Which?* magazine. Its purpose is to select a number of standards, make comparisons of these standards from item to item, and then reach logical conclusions and recommendations about which are the best and/or which represent the best value for money.

What points should I bear in mind?

It is essential to choose *sensible* standards and then to define them very carefully at the beginning of the report. Here are some standards important in any well-designed product:

♦ Does it work properly? A pop-up toaster should pop up toast.

♦ Is it fit for its purpose? A rewritable DVD should be rewritable.

♦ Can it cope with the likely conditions of use? A paper plate should be sturdy enough to hold food.

♦ Is it durable and easy to maintain for its expected lifespan? For example, are spare parts readily available?

♦ Is it safe and easy to use? A cooker should have no sharp edges and its controls should be clear.

◆ Is it pleasing to look at and to handle? Wallpaper must be attractive to potential customers.

◆ Does it have 'style'? A well-designed product combines a careful choice of colours, patterns and textures. It should be aesthetically pleasing.

Obviously the precise standards you choose will depend on the items being compared. Here are some examples of standards important when choosing a telephone:

◆ target price (comparing similar models)

◆ colour options

◆ features:

—last number redial
—number of memories
—a display
—battery back-up
—weight of handset
—maximum loudness of ring.

What would be a suitable format?

There are two basic ways of presenting these reports. The first is to define the first standard and then compare the performance of each item before moving on to the next standard. The second is to name the first item and then record how it matches up to various standards, before moving on to the next item.

There are three customary formats for comparative testing reports, as follows:

Comparison by Standard – Format A

1. Contents page
2. Introduction
3. Explanation and description of items to be compared
4. Comparison by Standard:

   Standard A
   - Item (i)
   - Item (ii)
   - Item (iii)

   Standard B
   - Item (i)
   - Item (ii)
   - Item (iii)

   Etc.

5. Conclusions
6. Recommendations.

Comparison by Standard – Format B

1. Contents page
2. Introduction
3. Summary of Standards and Data
4. Conclusions
5. Recommendations
6. Appendixes

(i) Explanation and description of items to be compared
(ii) Comparison by Standard A:
   - Explanation of Standard A
   - Comparison of items
(iii) Comparison by Standard B:
   - Explanation of Standard B
   - Comparison of items
   - Etc.

Comparison by Items

1. Contents page
2. Introduction
3. Explanation of Standards
4. Comparison by items:

   Item (i):
   - Standard A
   - Standard B
   - Standard C

   Item (ii):
   - Standard A
   - Standard B
   - Standard C

   Etc.

5. Conclusions
6. Recommendations.

If the comparison requires quite sophisticated technological investigation, you should also consider the use of formats B or C of **Technological Reports**.

DUTY NOTES REPORTS

See **Instructional Manuals.**

EXPLANATORY REPORTS

These are *factual* reports which provide an account of something that has happened.

What points should I bear in mind?

You must be unbiased and objective. Do not give any recommendations unless you are asked to do so.

What would be a suitable format?

This is a suitable format for an explanatory report:

1. Contents page
2. Introduction
   - Why was the report prepared, and who requested it?
   - Give a 'pen picture' of whatever has happened.
   - What is the position and authority of the writer?
3. Persons involved
   - Give their names and positions, where relevant.
4. Sequence of events
   - A simple, straightforward account of what happened.
5. Action taken
   - List all the critical actions taken in the order in which they occurred and the reasons for them. If necessary use appendices.
6. Cause and effect
   - What were the causes and effects of these actions?
7. Conclusions
   - How was the information for the report gathered?
   - How long did this take?
   - What degree of accuracy can the reader reasonably assume?
   - Are any important facts omitted?
   - If so, why?
8. Recommendations
   - If required.
9. Appendices
   - See section 5.

See also **Informative Reports**.

FEASIBILITY REPORTS

These discuss the practicality, and possibly the suitability and compatibility, of a given project, both in physical and economic terms. They also discuss the desirability of the proposed project from the viewpoint of those who would be affected by it. Report writers must come to a *conclusion*, and must *recommend* that some action is taken or is not taken and/or that some choice is adopted or is rejected.

What points should I bear in mind?

You must be unbiased and your approach must be logical. Be sure that you know the precise purpose of the proposed project and also its scope. See also **Systems Evaluation Reports**.

What would be a suitable format?

This is a suitable format for a feasibility report:

1. Abstract
2. Summary
3. Contents list (including a separate list of illustrations)
4. Glossary
5. Introduction (purpose and scope)
6. Discussion (the main body providing the evidence – use appendices if necessary)
7. Conclusions (flowing naturally from the discussion)
8. Recommendations (flowing naturally from the conclusions)
9. References, or Bibliography, or Resources (if necessary)
10. Appendices (see section 6).

Sometimes sections 1 and 2 are combined.

INFORMATIVE REPORTS

These are more general than explanatory reports (see above), but there is a degree of overlap. The purpose of an informative report is to increase the readers' knowledge of an event or to bring them up to date.

What points should I bear in mind?

You must present a clear overall theme. Each section of the report must be appropriate to this theme; there must be a good reason for including it. It is important to provide a logical plan because some readers may be interested in perhaps just one or two sections of the report.

What would be a suitable format?

This is a customary format for an informative report:

1. Contents page
2. Introduction (why was the report produced and what is hoped to be achieved by it?)
3. Plan (how the Main Body is structured)
4. Main Body (possibly one subsection for each main piece of information)
5. Conclusions (flowing naturally from the Main Body – also what, if anything, is it hoped will happen next?).

Sometimes sections 2 and 3 are combined. See also **Explanatory Reports**.

INSTRUCTIONAL MANUALS

Instructional manuals and duty notes are written to explain *how* a job or process (or perhaps how a particular aspect of a job or a process) is to be performed.

What points should I bear in mind?

Good instructional manuals and duty notes are written by people who know the job or process well. They know how much detailed instruction to include, and how much to leave out. Once you have drafted your instructions, try them out first on someone who is likely to use the report.

Do not confuse instructional manuals with **Process Description Reports**. As already stated, the former explain *how* a process is to be performed; the latter help the reader *understand* that process. So be absolutely sure of your purpose before deciding on a suitable format.

What would be a suitable format?

This is a typical format for an instructional manual or a set of duty notes:

1. Contents page
2. Job/Duty/Process objective (a brief statement of subject, purpose and scope)
3. Theory or principles of the operation (the mechanics of the process)
4. List of materials and equipment needed
5. Description of the mechanism (an overview of the equipment, possibly breaking it into its component parts)
6. List and number of steps necessary to complete the job
7. Instructions for each step (the main body)
8. Precautions necessary (explain why)
9. Show what must be done (use illustrations to support section 7)
10. The degree of difficulty at each stage.

Sections 3–5 and 8 are often omitted from clerical duty notes.

INTERVIEW REPORTS

Effective interviewing techniques are not within the scope of this book. However, a brief discussion on the preparation of interview reports is appropriate.

What points should I bear in mind?

Clear and adequate reports are essential to an interviewer who seeks a detailed and accurate recall and evaluation of interviewees (perhaps job applicants). Interviewers who lack the technique of interview report writing will merely attempt to rationalise their decision.

There are two types of interview report. The first is designed to ensure that an interview is well-structured, comprehensive, and that adequate and relevant notes are taken. The second is used to evaluate the material gathered during the interview.

What would be a suitable format?

The following format provides a useful framework for an interview. There will also be several sub-subheadings which are not given here. However the framework must be used with discretion. A good interview is **organic**, not mechanical.

A Structured Interview Report

1. Interviewee, interviewer, reference, date, time and location
2. Physical:
   – First impression
   – Appearance
   – Speech
   – Health
3. Attainments:
   – Work
   – Educational
   – Extramural

4. Interests
5. Circumstances:
   – Family background
   – Domestic and social situation.
6. Special aptitudes
7. General intelligence
8. Disposition.

After the interview the interviewer will need to evaluate the interviewees. This report format will be of assistance:

An Interview Evaluation Summary Report
1. Interviewee, interviewer, reference, date, time and location
2. Able to do
3. Willing to do:
   – Disposition
   – Motivation
4. Summary
5. Recommendation.

Before sections 2 and 3 can be completed the candidate will first be given a raw score of 1–5 (poor to outstanding) for every ability and willingness raised by the interviewer. However, as some of these qualities will be more important to the job than others, they will all be given a weighting, or relative importance score (often 1–7; useful to essential). The raw score will then be multiplied by the weighting, and the separate products will be totalled.

The top scorer is not necessarily the best candidate. For example, there may be a minimum total required for some or all the qualities, and these may not have all been met. However, this method does force the interviewer to think about the specific requirements of the job, and about how far the various interviewees meet them.

INVESTIGATION INTO THE FINANCIAL AFFAIRS OF A COMPANY REPORTS

There are numerous types of investigation – some private (for example, ones undertaken on behalf of a prospective purchaser of a business); others governed by statute (for example, reports for prospectuses and for Department of Trade investigations).

What points should I bear in mind?

In the case of a private investigation, the accountant must obtain precise instructions from his or her client (the terms of reference). In the case of an investigation governed by statute, the reporting accountant must be fully conversant with the statutory regulations, and must also obtain necessary instructions where applicable.

Throughout the investigation never lose sight of your purpose. It is all too easy to become side-tracked. First make preliminary inquiries to ascertain the information that is necessary to be able to plan the investigation. Draft a skeletal framework, detailing the headings which will be used in the final report. Then undertake all the necessary detailed work, recording your findings on working papers. From these the final report will be drafted.

What would be a suitable format?

This will depend on the nature of the investigation, but a typical structure is as follows:

1. Introduction (including the terms of reference and the nature and history of the enterprise being investigated)
2. Main body (the work performed and the facts ascertained – see below)
3. Conclusions (drawn from the main body)
4. Recommendations (drawn from the conclusions)
5. Appendixes (any voluminous statistics).

In the case of an investigation into a retail business on behalf of a potential purchaser, section 2 – the main body – could be subdivided as follows:

♦ 2.1 Management and Staff

♦ 2.2 Sales and Marketing

♦ 2.3 Purchases and Supplies

♦ 2.4 Trade Results (per audited accounts)

♦ 2.5 Prospects and Trends

♦ 2.6 Assets and Liabilities.

MINUTES

Minutes can be defined as a written record of the business transacted at a meeting. They may well have some legal and authoritative force.

What points should I bear in mind?

As a general rule, the fewer the words used the better. Ask yourself, what was the **purpose** of the meeting? Minutes of a formal meeting must include: decisions taken, motions passed and the names of the people who attended. Those of a **standing committee** must provide enough information and discussion so that absent members can participate on equal terms at the next meeting. Minutes of a **subcommittee** must include enough to keep its parent committee in touch with developments and to explain the reasons for decisions.

Write in the simple past tense (Mr Smith reported that . . .), and as soon as possible after the meeting. Selective note taking at the meeting will greatly assist this process. Concentrate on *conclusions*. Do not record controversy; state what was decided.

The way minutes are numbered varies from organisation to organisation. Here are three common methods:

♦ consecutively, from the first meeting onwards

♦ consecutively, beginning each set of minutes with ' 1'

♦ and consecutively, beginning each year with '1'.

Check that your minutes:

• provide a true, impartial and balanced account of the proceedings;

• are written in clear, concise and unambiguous language;

• are as concise as is compatible with the degree of accuracy required;

• follow a method of presentation which helps the reader assimilate the contents.

Once the minutes have been drafted, ask the chairperson to check them. Then circulate them to anyone who will be expected to act upon them. It is a good idea to clearly identify these people by putting their names in an 'action' column on the right of the page and opposite the appropriate references in the text.

If someone asks for a correction, try to negotiate an acceptable form of words. However do not be fooled by people who want you to report what they *should* have said, not what they *actually* said. At the following meeting these minutes will be discussed and any arguments over them will be resolved. The chairperson will then sign them as correct.

What would be a suitable format?

Headings in the minutes of a meeting should broadly correspond with those which appear in its agenda, as follows:

1. Heading (including where and when the meeting was held)
2. Present (who was there)
3. Apologies for Absence (who should have been there, but was not)
4. Minutes of the Previous Meeting (note any corrections and state 'The minutes were accepted as a true record of the meeting [with the above corrections]')
5. ⎫
6. ⎬ Simple statements of what actually occurred at the meeting
7. ⎪
8. ⎭
9. Any Other Business (the 'leftovers')
10. Date of Next Meeting (also give the time and location).

PROCESS DESCRIPTION REPORTS

A process is a specific series of actions that bring about a specific result.

What points should I bear in mind?

It is important not to confuse instructional manuals (see above) with process description reports. The former explain *how* a process is to be performed; the latter help the reader *understand* that process. Process description reports are used to describe the following:

♦   how something is made

♦   how something is done (for information, not instruction)

♦   how a mechanism works

♦   how a natural process occurs.

The report is essentially chronological or sequential and it is most commonly used within the world of business and industry. Almost every such report will include illustrations.

What would be a suitable format?

A suitable format for a process description report would be as follows:

1. Contents page (with a separate list of illustrations)
2. Introduction (identify the process; record its purpose and significance; give an overview of the steps involved)
3. Main body (discuss each step in turn)
4. Summary (concentrate on the purpose and importance of the actions or the significance of the facts).

PROGRESS REPORTS

These are periodic reports which, as their name suggests, describe how some activity or process is progressing. They are often built up from workers' daily logs, supervisors' reports, and so on.

What points should I bear in mind?

Progress reports will be required in one of three circumstances:

♦   on a regular basis

♦   at certain times during an activity or process, or

♦   as and when required.

They record progress over a specific period of time, and they make comparisons from period to period by identifying changes and their underlying causes and effects. They are essential for effective decision making so they must be clear, accurate and unambiguous.

What would be a suitable format?

Most organisations have standard printed progress report forms, although headings vary considerably. Here is one simple format:

1. Introduction
   - the period of work covered
   - the work planned
   - the authority for the work
   - the progress to date
2. Main Body
   - the work completed
   - how the work has been completed
   - the work planned for the future
   - an overall appraisal of the progress to date.

RESEARCH REPORTS

The purpose of a research report is to extend our understanding of the world by reducing uncertainty and increasing our comprehension of it.

What points should I bear in mind?

Results alone are never enough. As you will see from the typical format described below, you must be able to assess and then evaluate the *reliability* of the results. You must say precisely how the work was carried out, what methods were used to collect the data, and how it was analysed. Conclusions and recommendations must be drafted with great care.

What would be a suitable format?

This is a typical format for a research report:

1. Contents page
2. Introduction
   - Set the scene; give a clear statement of the objectives and scope of the research.

   – What was known about the subject at the beginning of the
     research?
   – Put the project into its proper context.
   – Give the reason(s) for the research.
   – Discuss the events which led up to it.
   – Assess the importance of other, related work.
3. Work carried out
   – Describe the overall shape and design of the research.
   – Describe the methods used (for example, sampling methods).
   – Describe the actual work carried out, probably in chronological
     order.
   – Explain how the results were analysed (for example, input to a
     computer).
4. The Results
   – In an academic report, give full results (with an interpretation in
     a separate section).
   – In a non-academic report, you can omit some results (or at least
     put them in an appendix) and emphasise significant results.
   – Concentrate on each objective of the research in turn.
   – Structure your results around these objectives.
   – Discuss the results; form links; build up an overall picture.
   – Distinguish 'facts' from interpretations, inferences, predictions
     or deductions.
5. Conclusions
   – Make sure they flow naturally from the results.
   – Each one must be supported by your findings and/or other
     research.
   – If no clear picture has emerged, then say so.
   – Do not see relationships that do not exist.
6. Recommendations
   – These should flow naturally from your conclusions, with no
     surprises.

7. Appendixes
   – Include items which would disturb the flow of the report (for example, survey forms and questionnaires).
8. References, or Bibliography, or Resources.

SCIENTIFIC REPORTS

A scientific report consists of an account of a test or experiment, of its findings, and of its conclusions.

What points should I bear in mind?
Before you can write the report, you must carry out the test or experiment accurately and you must record your results as you proceed. Here are some points to bear in mind:

♦ Make sure you understand the purpose of the test or experiment.

♦ If you are not familiar with the relevant theory, look it up before you start.

♦ Make sure you select appropriate equipment with reference to its accuracy, sensitivity and safety. Ensure you know how the equipment works, and then set it up in the most sensible way for you to make all the required measurements and observations.

♦ Carry out the test or experiment, recording *every* observation as you proceed. Ensure you observe and record accurately.

♦ Always record the units of measurement. All readings must be consistent, for example to two decimal places.

♦ There is no point in giving a reading of, say, 0.2317mm unless you have a good reason to believe that it lies somewhere between 0.231 and 0.232mm. If you do not have good reason to believe this, then record the result only to the degree of precision to which you have confidence – perhaps 0.23mm.

♦ Record the estimated limits of error. If a spring can measure with an accuracy of plus or minus 0.1mm, you should record this as, say,

$$\text{length of spring} = 21.7 \pm 0.1\text{mm}$$

♦ If you add a mass to the spring and re-measure, the error could be plus or minus 0.1mm on both figures; so record this as, say,

$$\text{change of length of spring} = 14.9 \pm 0.2\text{mm}$$

♦ Calculate the results and draw any necessary rough graphs in pencil. If the results are unreasonable or inconsistent (out of line), then make the tests again.

♦ Form a conclusion based on your accumulated evidence.

♦ Write the report.

What would be a suitable format?

This is the usual format for a scientific report:

1. Name of class, group or department; experiment number; reference; date and time
   - The time is relevant only if it is likely to affect results (for example, was barometric pressure a factor?).
2. Title of experiment.
3. Summary (or Abstract or Synopsis)
   - A brief statement about the structure of the report; why the experiment was carried out; what you found, and the significance of what you found.
4. Contents page.
5. Introduction
   - Your purpose and scope.
6. Apparatus
   - A list of apparatus and details of its arrangements, with diagrams.

7. Circuit theory
   - Where applicable. A brief account of the theory underlying the experiment.
8. Method
   - A full and clear account of how the experiment was carried out. Write in the passive (A glass stopper was weighed).
9. Results (or Findings)
   - All your readings neatly tabulated with graphs neatly drawn. Give the estimated limits of error (see above). If necessary use appendixes.
10. Conclusion (or Discussion)
    - The inferences drawn from the results obtained (these results show . . .). Interpret results and explain their significance.
    - Could this experiment have been improved in some way? If so, explain why and how.
11. Appendixes
    - To support section 9, if necessary.

STUDENT PROJECT REPORTS

Many students are required to undertake projects and produce reports. For example, they are an important part of many GCSE examination schemes.

What points should I bear in mind?
Here are some points to bear in mind when carrying out a project:

♦ Be aware of who will choose the topic. It may be chosen by your teacher, or by you, or through discussion between the two of you.

♦ The topic chosen must be acceptable to your examining group. So talk to your teacher and refer to your syllabus. Then select a suitable topic, preferably one that can be investigated locally.

♦ Decide what sources of information you will require.

♦ Decide how you will gather this information.

♦ Gather the information.

♦ Analyse the information.

♦ Write the report.

What would be a suitable format?

If your teacher or lecturer tells you the required format, or if it is given in your syllabus, comply with it. If you have no such instruction or guidance, consider this simple format:

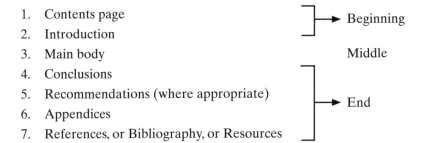

1. Contents page
2. Introduction   → Beginning
3. Main body   Middle
4. Conclusions
5. Recommendations (where appropriate)
6. Appendices   → End
7. References, or Bibliography, or Resources

See also **Technological Reports**.

SYSTEMS EVALUATION REPORTS

A systems evaluation report serves one of these purposes:

♦ To discover which system out of several alternatives is most suitable for a particular application.

♦ To test an apparatus or system which it is intended to employ on a large scale, or with multiple applications, if the initial operation is deemed worthwhile.

♦ To enquire into the causes of failures in an existing operational system.

The last of these is considered under **Trouble-Shooting Reports**.

What points should I bear in mind?

The purpose of the first two types of report is to inform those concerned with selection, implementation and utilisation about:

♦ the requirements of the application

♦ the criteria by which the systems should be judged

♦ the features of available systems

♦ data on their performance in the field

♦ and recommendations or conclusions about the best course of action.

These reports are important – mistakes are costly. You must be independent; do not rely on the word of manufacturers or suppliers. You probably will need to use supplementary text, footnotes, a glossary and illustrations (diagrams, flow charts and perhaps photographs).

What would be a suitable format?

A suitable format for a report with the purpose of discovering which system out of several alternatives is most suitable for a particular application is as follows:

1. Contents page
2. Preface (personal background: why have you written the report?)
3. System Requirements
4. Systems Available
5. Criteria for Selection

6. The Final Choice
7. Appendices (System Data Sheets).

A report on the initial performance of an apparatus or a system could follow this format:

1. Contents page
2. Preface (personal background: why have you written the report?)
3. Apparatus/System Requirements
4. Apparatus/System Performance (use appendices, if necessary)
5. Conclusions
6. Recommendation
7. Appendices (to support section 4, if necessary).

See also **Feasibility Reports** and **Trouble-Shooting Reports**.

TECHNICAL REPORTS

Technical reports are often written at an early stage in a production process. They are usually generated internally, either by the technical publications department of an organisation or by staff involved in this production process. Here are some examples of technical reports:

♦ a technical proposal

♦ a feasibility study

♦ design and research reports

♦ pre-production reports

♦ evaluation documents

♦ ad hoc reports.

What points should I bear in mind?

These reports are often written by engineers who are not always familiar with the techniques of effective writing. The advice given throughout this book, therefore, will be of assistance.

What would be a suitable format?

Every organisation will have its own format requirements. This is a typical layout:

1. Contents page
2. Aims (why it was written, its terms of reference and its general purpose)
3. Summary (the salient facts and a concise summary of conclusions, if any)
4. Main body (main discussion of the subject matter)
5. Conclusions (if necessary)
6. References, or Bibliography, or Resources (if required)
7. Index (in larger reports only).

TECHNOLOGICAL REPORTS

A technological report is concerned with the application of practical or mechanical sciences in order to achieve a desired aim.

What points should I bear in mind?

A good technological report should combine and *demonstrate* these qualities:

♦   planning

♦   communication

♦   ability to reason

- ability to evaluate

- a logical and realistic solution.

Show the 'thinking' that has gone into the report. Make sure it is well organised and well-presented. Present it logically to show a well-constructed development of the problem-solving process. Reach a solution which achieves your objective. Evaluate your work: are you satisfied with it? Is it economically viable?

What would be a suitable format?

Here are three formats. As always, select the one that best suits your needs:

Format A

1. Contents page
2. Brief (what you were attempting to do)
3. Analysis (your analysis of the problem – include the research material you have gathered)
4. Thinking (your initial thinking and your evaluation of it)
5. Solution (explain how you developed your solution)
6. Evidence (include drawings, photographs and other evidence of your solution – the artefact)
7. Evaluation (an objective evaluation of your solution).

This format would be suitable for a Student Project Report about the production of an artefact (a physical thing created by one or more human beings, such as a working model or a piece of woodwork).

Format B

1. Contents page
2. Purpose
   – why was the work undertaken?

3. Methods Used
   - the apparatus and equipment used (with illustrations)
   - a step-by-step account of the procedure
   - observations taken (tabulated) – use appendices, if necessary
   - calculations necessary to give meaning to the observations
4. Results
   - use tables and illustrations (and appendices, if necessary)
5. Conclusions
   - a survey of the work undertaken:
     - compare actual results with theoretical results
     - compare actual results with others obtained elsewhere
     - give reasons for such discrepancies or variations
     - assess the relevance of the methods used
     - assess the efficiency of the equipment used
     - discuss any human errors and/or any relevant environmental factors
6. Recommendations
   - flowing naturally from your conclusions
7. Appendices
   - to support sections 3 and/or 4, if necessary.

Format C
1. Contents page
2. Summary
   - concentrate on your findings
3. Object
   - a brief statement of your aim
4. Introduction
   - why was the work undertaken?
   - provide any relevant background information
   - discuss any limitations/conditions you faced (for example: cost, time, or environmental)

5. Apparatus
   - describe it (with illustrations)
   - why was it chosen?
6. Procedures
   - a step-by-step account of what was done
7. Observations
   - give details of components, specimens, equipment or machinery during and after the test
   - record the readings made during the investigation in tables and/ or illustrations – use appendices, if necessary
8. Calculations
   - based on your observations
   - based on theoretical considerations
   - analyse errors
   - summarise your results
9. Results
   - use a separate section or appendix, if necessary
10. Comments
    - discuss the degree of accuracy achieved
    - compare your results with those from other sources
    - comment on quality of the materials and workmanship of the item tested
    - what alternative method(s) of presenting your findings could you have used?
    - why did you present your findings as you have?
    - make your acknowledgements
11. Conclusions
    - flowing from your results and, where appropriate, your comments
12. Recommendations
    - flowing from your conclusions
13. Appendices
    - to support sections 7 and/or 9, if necessary

14. Index
    – in larger reports only.

Formats B and C are suitable for technological tests or investigations, perhaps assessing the suitability of two or more items for a defined purpose. Format C is particularly useful for a long report. See also **Comparative Testing Reports**.

TROUBLE-SHOOTING REPORTS

These reports aim to locate the cause of some problem, and then suggest ways to remove or treat it. In the main they deal with people, organisations or hardware.

What points should I bear in mind?

These reports highlight problems. When they are caused by people you must be especially careful to word the report thoughtfully. Be candid but be fair. Most of all, be accurate. When you are discussing problems caused by the structure of an organisation, you must expect to meet the objection: 'But we've always done it this way'. People are generally not keen on change. Reports on hardware are less complicated and often less contentious.

What would be a suitable format?

Here are four possible structures. Choose the one that best suits your needs:

Format A
1. Contents page
2. Present situation (the salient points)
3. Options for Change (the pros and cons of each option)
4. Recommendations (well-argued, clear, unambiguous and concise)
5. References, or Bibliography, or Resources (if required).

Format B

1. Contents page
2. Introduction (purpose and scope)
3. Evidence (concise, balanced and unambiguous – use appendices, if necessary)
4. Arguments for (present all the pros logically and objectively and respond positively to weaknesses in your case)
5. Arguments against (list them and refute them in turn)
6. Recommendation (be clear, unambiguous and precise)
7. Appendices (to support section 3, if necessary)
8. References, or Bibliography, or Resources (if required).

Format C

1. Contents page
2. Introduction (your purpose)
3. Summary of Recommendations (clear, unambiguous and precise)
4. Present Position (the salient points)
5. Scope (what work was done, and possibly what was not)
6. Observations on Recommendations (the main body – repeat each recommendation and give the main pros and cons for each – say why the pros prevailed)
7. Conclusion (keep it concise)
8. Appendices (if required)
9. References, or Bibliography, or Resources (if required).

Format D

1. Contents page
2. The Problem
   – nature and cause
   – extent
   – effects (perhaps on safety or production)
3. The Need for Change
   – reasons (perhaps labour problems or competition)
4. Proposed Solution

- options available
- details of proposed solution
- previous experience of this scheme (perhaps elsewhere)
- advantages
- disadvantages (and how they can be overcome)
- effects (perhaps improved efficiency or sales prospects)

5. Time Factors
   - when can it be implemented?
6. Costs
   - for *each* option:
   - implementation costs
   - running costs
   - estimated savings, if applicable
7. Conclusion
   - for the *chosen* option:
   - overall effects
   - overall benefits
8. Recommendations
   - item by item, clear and unambiguous
9. Appendices
   - if required
10. References, or Bibliography, or Resources
    - if required.

See also **Feasibility Reports** and **Systems Evaluation Report**.

Appendix 1
Harvard Referencing

In any report where you include the work of others to *support* your own work, it is essential to give due credit to these sources and authors. Citation and referencing is a system that allows you to indicate where you have referred to ideas, theories, quotations, statistics and other information which were originally produced by someone else. It also allows your readers to refer to these sources directly, if they wish.

It is important to recognise that there is no one universally accepted method of citing and referencing, so you should always refer to previous reports produced within your organisation, or consult the person who commissioned or requested your report to be absolutely sure of the system that *you* are expected to employ. What follows is an outline of how to cite and reference using the Harvard method, a system employed in many academic reports.

CITING IN THE TEXT

A citation in the text should provide basic details of your source. In the case of books and journals these would be the author's name, date of publication and page numbers (if appropriate). There are a number of ways in which citations can be given simply and unobtrusively without interrupting the flow of your report. Here are a few examples:

> Williams (2005) disagrees fundamentally with Davis (1999), arguing that . . .

The case for a total ban is made persuasively by Woodbine (2011, p 69).

An alternative approach is proposed by Chick (2003).

Such citations are usually written in the *present tense*, even though the books or other sources may have been published some time ago. Another point to note is that it should always be possible to remove a pair of brackets containing a publication date without disturbing the sense and grammatical accuracy of the remaining sentence. For example:

Williams disagrees fundamentally with Davis, arguing that . . .

From the basic details you provide within the text, your readers will be able to locate the full details of the items you have used by looking through the alphabetical list of referenced material towards the end of your report. For example:

Citation in the Main Body or Appendices:

There is a strong case for believing that some Latin American countries are unlikely to become full democracies for at least 50 years (Peeler, 2004, p 146).

Corresponding reference in References, or in the Bibliography or Resources section:

Peeler, J., 2004. *Building democracy in Latin America.* 2nd ed. Boulder: Lynne Rienner.

When you need to cite a work written by two authors, each should be credited:

Jackson and Miller (2011) form the view that . . .

If there are three or more authors, the convention is to give the first author's surname followed by the Latin phrase for *and others*:

Armitage *et al* (2003) conclude that . . .

If you need to cite two or more documents published by the same writer and in the same year, distinguish them by adding lower case letters after the year within the brackets. For example:

Lewis (2004 a) estimates that over 50% of purchasers are strongly influenced by . . .
and later in report

This will cause manufacturers to seek alternative suppliers (Lewis, 2004 b).

If more than one citation is referred to within the same sentence, each essentially in agreement, list them in the following form: by date – most recent first – and then alphabetically:

There are strong indications that passive smoking is threatening to health . . . (Letwin, 2011; Casey, 2009; Brown, 2007; Robinson 2007).

If you are quoting directly from a text, you must use inverted commas. If the quote is more than two lines long then it should be separated from the main body of your work by *indenting* it. The page number(s) must also be included. For example:

Thomas and Ingham (1995), when discussing staff development, comment that:

'Development is infectious, and staff who previously have recoiled from undertaking a degree or conversion course have been encouraged by the success of others' (p 33).

This finding is reinforced by the work of . . .

REFERENCING YOUR MATERIALS

All sources cited within the text must also be referenced on a separate page (or pages) at the end of your report. These should be listed in alphabetical order, by the author's surname, and recorded in the forms shown below:

Reference to a book: one author:

Author's Surname, INITIALS., year of publication. *Title*. edition (if not the first) Place of publication: Publisher. For example:

> Godsmark, C., 2010. *Start and run a business*. Oxford: How To Books.

Reference to a book: two authors:

Author's Surname, INITIALS., and Author's Surname, INITIALS., year of publication. *Title*. edition (if not the first) Place of publication: Publisher. For example:

> Herrmann, C., and Terhechte, J.P., 2011. *European yearbook of economic law*. Berlin: Springer Medizin.

Reference to a book: three or more authors:

1st Author's Surname, INITIALS., 2nd (and subsequent) Author's Surname, INITIALS., and last Author's Surname, INITIALS., year of publication. *Title*. edition (if not the first) Place of publication: Publisher. For example:

> Beith, L., Pullan, L., and Robinson, M., 2003. *Early years care and education (level 2)*. London: Heinemann Educational Publishers.

Reference to a contribution in a book:

Contributor's Surname, INITIALS., year of publication. Title of contribution. In: Surname, INITIALS of author (or editor) of Publication., (followed by ed. or eds if appropriate). *Title of book*. Place of publication: Publisher, page numbers of contribution. For example:

> Saso, M., 1997. Chinese religions. *In*: Hinnells, J., ed. *The new Penguin handbook of living religions*. London: Penguin, pp 445-478.

If there is more than one contributor, each should be identified, as in the author examples above.

Reference to a book: editor:

Editor's Surname, INITIALS., ed., year of publication. *Title*. edition (if not the first). Place of publication: Publisher. For example:

> Danaher, P., ed., 1998. *Beyond the ferris wheel*. Rockampton: CQU Press.

If there is more than one editor, each should be identified, as in the author examples above. Additionally, the initials of each should be immediately followed by ', ed.,'.

Reference to a publication from a corporate body (such as a government department or other organisation):

Name of Issuing Body, year of publication. *Title of publication*. Place of publication: Publisher, Report Number (where relevant). For example:

> Office for National Statistics, 2012. *Social Trends*. London: Palgrave Macmillan.

Reference to an article in a journal (paper format/hard copy):

Author's Surname, INITIALS., year of publication. Title of article, *Title of Journal*, Volume number and (part number), page numbers of contribution. For example:

> Feldman, H.N., 1993. Maternal care and differences in the use of nests by the domestic cat. *Animal Behaviour*, 45 (1), pp 13–23.

Reference to an article in a journal, downloaded from a database:

Author's Surname, INITIALS., year of publication. Title of article. *Title of Journal*, Volume number and (part number), page number(s). Available from: Uniform Resource Locator (URL) of source/database. (Accessed date). For example:

> Nicholson, R., 1999. The blackest flower in the world. *Natural History*, 108 (4), p 60. Available from http://galegroup.com. (Accessed 20 December 2011).

Reference to a newspaper article in paper format:

Author's Surname, INITIALS., year of publication. Title of article. *Title of Newspaper*, Day and Month, page number(s) and column number. For example:

> Sharrock, D., 2008. Newspaper that slated 'joyless' restaurant wins appeal over libel. *The Times*. 11 March, 24a.

Reference to a newspaper article from a database:

Author's Surname, INITIALS., year of publication. Title of article. *Title of Newspaper*, Day and Month, page number(s) and column number. Available from: URL of source/database. (Accessed date). For example:

> Hughes. F., 2008. Chilling Memories (features). *The Times*, 10 March, p 2. Available from: http://galegroup.com. (Accessed 17 June 2011).

Reference to web documents and e-books in PDF documents:

Author's/Editor's Surname, INITIALS., year. *Title.* Edition, if not the first. Place of publication: Publisher (if ascertainable). Available from: URL (Accessed date). For example:

> Crofts, A., and Jefferson, R.G., eds. 1999. *The lowland grassland management handbook.* 2nd ed. London: Royal Society for Nature Conservation. Available from: http://naturalengland.communisis. com/naturalenglandshop/docs/low00front.pdf (Accessed 18 January 2012).

Reference to web pages/sites in HTML format:

Author's/Editor's Surname, INITIALS., year. *Title.* Place of publication: Publisher (if ascertainable). Available from: URL (Accessed date). For example:

> Natural England, 2008. *Science, research and evidence.* London: Natural England. Available from: http://www.english-nature.org. uk/science (Accessed 9 October 2011).

Reference to a DVD, video, film or broadcast:

Title, year (for films the preferred date is the year of release in the country of production). Material designation. Subsidiary originator (optional but director is preferred). Production details – place: organisation. For example:

> *Inception*, 2010. Film. Directed by Christopher Nolan. UK: Warner.

Reference to a television programme and series:

Series Title, number of series. number of episode (cumulative episode number, if known), title of episode, year. Material designation, transmitting organisation, channel. Date of transmission. For example:

> *Upstairs Downstairs*, 5.16 (68), Whither shall I wander?, TV, ITV. 21 December 1975.

Reference to a podcast:

Broadcaster's/Author's Surname, INITIALS., year. *Programme title*, Series Title (if relevant) (type of medium) date of transmission. Available from: include website address/URL (Accessed date). For example:

> National Gallery, 2008, *Episode seventeen*, The National Gallery Monthly Podcast. (podcast) March 2008. Available from: http://www.nationalgallery.org.uk/podcasts (Accessed 29 October 2011).

Reference to email correspondence:

It is important to seek permission before reproducing an email, especially if the email address is to be included in the citation and reference.

Sender's Surname, INITIALS., email address, year. *Message or subject title from posting line.* (type of medium) Message to Recipient's Surname, INITIALS., (recipient's email address). Day and Date sent, including time. Available from: URL (for example where the message is archived). (Accessed date). For example:

> Chapman, S., schapman@chapman.com, 2011. *Uninteresting interest rates.* (email) Message to Mcbride, A., (amcbride@anytown. ac.uk). Sent Monday 20 December, 2011, 09.16. Available from: http://gog.defer.com/2009-08-01-defer-archive.htm (Accessed 20 December 2011).

Reference to blogs:

Comment Author's Surname, INITIALS., year. Title of individual blog entry. *Blog title*, (medium) Blog posting date. Available from: include website address URL (Accessed date). For example:

> Whitton, F., 2009. Conservationists are not making themselves heard. *Guardian.co.uk Science blog* (blog) 18 June. Available from:

http://www.guardian.co.uk/science/blog2009/jun18/consevation-extinction-open-ground (Accessed 23 June 2011).

Reference to social network sites (such as Facebook or Twitter):
Author's Surname, INITIALS., year *Title of page*. (Title of website). Day/Month of posted message. Available from: web address. (Accessed date). For example,

Owen, J., 2012 *Referencing Group*. (Facebook). 12 February. Available from: www.facebook.com. (Accessed 18 February 2012).

Appendix 2
Sample Reports

Here are excerpts from three recent BMA reports, written in differing styles reflecting their differing purposes and target readerships.

The first report was published in 2009 and is concerned with the treatment of healthcare associated infections (HCAIs).

Overleaf is the contents page which shows the overall structure of the report. This is followed by the introduction which clearly sets the scene and effectively engages the readers' interest.

The report is intended primarily for policy makers with strategic or operational responsibility for public health in the UK, although it will also be of interest to healthcare professionals and patients.

TACKLING HEALTHCARE ASSOCIATED INFECTIONS THROUGH EFFECTIVE POLICY ACTION

Contents

INTRODUCTION

Over the past two decades, HCAIs have become a significant challenge, both in terms of the risk to patient wellbeing, as well as the cost to the NHS. This has been accompanied by intense media and public attention, to the extent that the prevention and control of infections is now a key focus for healthcare policy in the UK. Despite this, efforts to tackle the problem have focused primarily on reducing rates of meticillin-resistant *Staphylococcus aureus* (*S. aureus*, MRSA) bacteraemia and *Clostridium difficile* (*C. difficile*) infection. Much less attention has been paid to other types of HCAIs, including infections acquired in primary and community healthcare settings.

Hospitalisation and interventions for the purposes of healthcare have always been associated with a risk of infection. Advances in medical technology and treatment, however, have meant that more patients are being treated than ever before, and many are increasingly vulnerable to infections due to a greater severity of underlying illness, the use of invasive procedures, and as a result of suppression of the immune system. This has been compounded by rising levels of resistance as pathogens adapt to exposure to antimicrobial agents, as well as organisational factors such as high bed occupancy and understaffing. The risk of acquiring an infection is therefore dependent on a complex interplay between micro-organisms, patients, healthcare workers, visitors, and the environment. Not all HCAIs can be prevented; however, high standards of infection control can minimise the risk of occurrence.

Healthcare associated infections affect patients in a variety of ways, from increased discomfort and pain to severe illness, permanent disability and in some cases, death. Infection also leads to extended stays for affected patients, bed and ward closure, and increased diagnostic and treatment costs. The prevention and control of HCAIs is therefore essential. Reducing the burden of HCAIs requires commitment from all healthcare professionals, patients, and visitors as well as strong leadership at an organisational and national level.

This report considers the problems associated with HCAIs and examines the patterns and trends of these infections in the UK. It goes on to review the evidence base for the range of infection control policies, and identifies areas that require action in order to reduce the burden of HCAIs.

*   *   *

This second report is concerned with equality and diversity in UK medical schools. In recent decades, the student composition has changed with regards to the age, ethnicity and gender of students.

The report, which was also published in 2009, outlines the current demography of medical schools, highlights important questions for discussion and identifies areas which would benefit from further research. It is informative in nature and is intended to form a basis for debate and future policy decisions.

Age is an increasingly important issue in medical education. In recent years, graduate entry to medical school has become more common, while at the same time new legislation against age discrimination makes universities' responsibilities more complex. Section 3 of the report explores these key issues for the discipline of medical education. What follows is a summary of these findings followed by a series of questions which need to be addressed.

The UK medical profession is notable for its ethnic diversity, yet challenges remain in preventing discrimination and ensuring equality of opportunity for all. Section 4 explores this issue. Again findings are clearly summarised and key questions are proposed.

EQUALITY AND DIVERSITY IN UK MEDICAL SCHOOLS
SECTION 3: AGE

Summary

A higher proportion of applicants under the age of 21 receive acceptances compared to other age groups; mature applicants sometimes appear to be at a disadvantage. At the same time, the past decade has seen a definite shift in the age pattern of medical students, so that about one in five students accepted into medical degrees is now aged 21 or over. This suggests that medical schools may be adopting a more favourable attitude towards older applicants. This changing demography of medical schools may be due partly to the effect of graduate-entry programmes, new medical schools and access courses, all of which have helped to reduce barriers to medical school faced by older students. There are several perceived advantages of admitting mature students to medical school, such as better developed communications skills and capacity to deal with others. There is little conclusive research, however, on the differences in outcome between older and more traditional students. Mature and graduate students still face problems in entering medicine, including financial barriers.

Questions for discussion

♦ Why is the acceptance rate of applicants aged under 21 higher than in any other age group?

♦ What is the optimal age range for entry to medical school?

♦ Should the UK increase the number of graduate-entry students?

♦ Why are all medical schools not offering graduate entry and widening access courses?

SECTION 4: ETHNICITY

Summary

Medicine attracts a higher proportion of ethnic minority students when compared to the general university population. This proportion seems to have remained relatively stable in recent years. There are large differences in the acceptance rates among the different ethnic groups. This could be due to factors including educational differences, social class and direct or indirect discrimination. In the case of ethnicity it appears to be especially important that medical schools' selection and assessment processes are evaluated and made as transparent, fair and objective as possible. It is also crucial to ensure that discrimination does not reduce the chances of success at medical school for ethnic minority students.

Questions for discussion

♦ What are the best ways of raising expectations among pupils from under-represented minority ethnic groups to encourage them to apply for medical school?

♦ How can the ethnicity of medical school applicants and acceptances be monitored most robustly?

♦ What are the most important steps that should be taken to ensure equality of opportunity in medical schools?

♦ Why do some minority ethnic groups (for example, Black-African) have a significantly lower acceptance rate compared to applicants from other ethnic origins?

*   *   *

This final report, published in 2008, is concerned with the problematic levels of alcohol misuse in the UK. It examines the patterns and trends of alcohol consumption and goes on to review the range of adverse effects, both on the individual and society, which are associated with its misuse.

The report concludes by considering evidence for effective alcohol control policies and discusses current approaches in the UK. The recommendations for action by the UK Government – some of which are reproduced here – are evidence-based policies that need to be adopted in order to tackle alcohol misuse and its associated harm.

ALCOHOL MISUSE: TACKLING THE UK EPIDEMIC
RECOMMENDATIONS

Access to alcohol – controlling price and availability

♦ Taxation on all alcoholic beverages should be increased at higher than inflation rates and this increase should be proportionate to the amount of alcohol in the product.

♦ The availability of alcoholic products should be regulated through a reduction in licensing hours for on- and off-licensed premises.

♦ Town planning and licensing authorities should ensure they consider the local density of on-licensed premises and the surrounding infrastructure when evaluating any planning or licensing application. Legislative changes should be introduced where necessary to ensure these factors are considered in planning or licensing applications for licensed premises.

Responsible retailing and industry practices

♦ Licensing legislation in the UK should be strictly and rigorously enforced. This includes the use of penalties for breach of licence, suspension or removal of licences, the use of test purchases to monitor underage sales, and restrictions on individuals with a history of alcohol-related crime or disorder.

♦ Enforcement agencies should be adequately funded and resourced so that they can effectively carry out their duties. Consideration should be given to the establishment of a dedicated alcohol licensing and inspection service.

♦ Legislation should be introduced throughout the UK to:
  – prohibit irresponsible promotional activities in licensed premises and by off-licences
  – set minimum price levels for the sale of alcoholic beverages.

♦ A statutory code of practice on the marketing of alcoholic beverages should be introduced and rigorously enforced. This should include a ban on:
  – broadcasting of alcohol advertising at any time that is likely to be viewed prior to 9pm and in cinemas before films with a certificate below age 18
  – alcohol industry sponsorship of sporting, music and other entertainment events aimed mainly at young people
  – marketing of alcoholic soft drinks to young people.

Measures to reduce drink-driving

♦ The legal limit for the level of alcohol permitted while driving, attempting to drive, or being in charge of a vehicle should be reduced from 80mg/100ml to 50mg/100ml throughout the UK.

♦ Legislation permitting the use of random roadside testing without the need for prior suspicion of intoxication should be introduced throughout the UK. This requires appropriate resourcing and public awareness campaigns.

Education and health promotion

♦ There should be further qualitative research examining attitudes to alcohol misuse in the UK.

♦ Public and school-based alcohol educational programmes should only be used as part of a wider alcohol-related harm reduction strategy to support policies that have been shown to be effective at altering drinking behaviour, to raise awareness of the adverse effects of alcohol misuse, and to promote public support for comprehensive alcohol control measures.

♦ It should be a legal requirement to:
 a) prominently display a common standard label on all alcoholic products that clearly states:
  – alcohol content in units
  – recommended daily UK guidelines for alcohol consumption
  – a warning message advising that exceeding these guidelines may cause the individual and others harm.

 b) include in all printed and electronic alcohol advertisements information on:
  – recommended daily UK guidelines for alcohol consumption
  – a warning message advising that exceeding these guidelines may cause the individual and others harm.

♦ It should be a legal requirement for retailers to prominently display at all points where alcoholic products are for sale:
 – information on recommended daily UK guidelines for alcohol consumption
 – a warning message advising that exceeding these guidelines may cause the individual and others harm.

Glossary

Abstract (or **Summary**, or **Synopsis**). A condensed version of a report which outlines the salient points and emphasises the main **conclusions** (*qv*) and, where appropriate, the main **recommendations** (*qv*). It has two functions: either to provide a précis of what the recipient is about to read, or has just read; or to provide a summary of a report if the recipient is not going to read all of it.

Acknowledgements. An author's statement of thanks to people and organisations who helped during the preparation of a report.

Addendum (*pl.* **Addenda**). Additional material; an update or afterthought often produced and circulated after a report has been issued.

Agenda. A type of report listing items to be discussed during a meeting. Therefore it must be drawn up in advance.

Aims. A statement of why a report was written; who requested it, when it was requested; and its **terms of reference** (*qv*). It usually appears in the **introduction** (*qv*).

Algorithm. A **flowchart** (*qv*) which will answer a question, or solve a problem, or undertake a procedure within a finite number of steps.

Annual Report. A type of report which lists the achievements and failures of an organisation; a **progress report** (*qv*) in which every department is accounted for.

Appendix (*pl.* **Appendixes** or **Appendices**). A section of a report which gives details of matters discussed more broadly in the **main body** (*qv*). It provides additional information for readers who require it without breaking the thread of argument in the main body for readers who do not.

Appraisal report. A type of report which evaluates a person's performance in his or her current job; identifies methods of improving this performance; and often assesses suitability for another job, promotion and/or a change in salary.

Artwork. The images in a report, such as **clip art** (*qv*), original art or photographs.

Audit report. An external audit report is addressed to shareholders and contains an independent assessment of whether a company's final statements provide a true and fair view of its affairs. An internal audit report is addressed to the management of a company by which the auditor is employed, and is more concerned with segregation of duties and internal control.

Bar chart. A method of presenting figures visually. Very useful for illustrating relationships between items.

Bias. Errors that occur in **statistical sampling** (*qv*) if the sample is not **random** (*qv*) or if the questioning is not objective and consistent. See **Leading question**.

Bibliography. A full list of books and other material used in the preparation of a report. Unlike a reference section, it may also include publications not referred to in the report, but considered potentially valuable or of interest to readers – *cf* **References** and **Resources**.

Binding. The process of assembling the pages of a report in order and then enclosing them within covers.

Bitmap. A computer image, like a colour photograph – *cf* **Vector**.

Bulleting. A method of **highlighting** (*qv*) important text by **indenting** (*qv*) it and placing a bold dot or bullet in front of the first word.

Caption (or **Legend**, or **Underline**). Descriptive words or lines accompanying an **illustration** (*qv*).

Centring text. A method of refining the appearance of **text** (*qv*) where each line is placed centrally between the right and left margins. This can be used for whole blocks of text but is more frequently applied to **headings** (*qv*).

Circulation list. See **Distribution list**.

Citations. Short, basic acknowledgements of **sources** (*qv*) provided within the **text** (*qv*) – *cf* **References**.

Clip art illustrations (*qv*) available commercially in digital form.

Column. A **format** (*qv*) using one, two, or three vertical groupings on a page.

Comparative testing report. A type of report which tests similar items, assessing each against a number of well-defined standards, and reaching logical **conclusions** (*qv*) and **recommendations** (*qv*) about which are the best and/or which represent the best value for money. The Consumers' Association *Which?* magazine contains such reports.

Components. The various sections which collectively make up a report.

Conclusions. A section of a report where the author links the **terms of reference** (*qv*) with the findings, as presented in the **main body** (*qv*), and reaches clear, simply stated and objective **conclusions** (*qv*) that are fully supported by evidence and arguments and which come within and satisfy the **terms of reference** (*qv*).

Confidentiality. The degree to which the availability of a report is restricted. Reports are often classified as confidential when they contain politically or industrially sensitive information or comment, or when they discuss personnel. Confidential reports should be stamped as such on the **title page** (*qv*) and should be kept under physically secure conditions.

Contact point. The name, address and telephone number of a person the reader can contact if further enquiry or comment is required. It should be given in a report's **covering letter** (*qv*).

Contents page. A list of the various sections of a report in the order in which they appear, with the appropriate page and/or paragraph numbers alongside them. If there are more than just one or two **illustrations** (*qv*) they should be listed separately below the main contents, giving their **captions** (*qv*), figure numbers and page and/or paragraph numbers.

Copyright. Legal protection against the use of literary or artistic property without permission. The protection afforded by English law lasts for the duration of the author's life and seventy years thereafter. Copyright is different from a patent in that it cannot exist in an idea, but only in its expression.

Covering letter. An explanatory letter accompanying a report and including a **contact point** (*qv*).

Creative substructure. A **substructure** (*qv*) where information is presented in an apparently haphazard way. A hybrid of the **logical substructure** (*qv*) and the **sectional substructure** (*qv*).

Cross-reference. A method of directing readers to another part of a report for related information.

Cut-away drawing. A pictorial method of illustrating what something looks like. An object is shown with part or all of its outer casing cut away to reveal its internal components.

Desktop Publishing (DTP). The use of a personal computer system as an inexpensive production system for generating typeset-quality **text** (*qv*) and **graphics** (*qv*). Desktop publishers often merge text and graphics on the same page and print pages on a high resolution laser printer or typesetting machine – *cf* **Word processing**.

Digital. A **format** (*qv*) used by a computer system that scans the image into computer bits.

Distribution list (or **Circulation list**). A list of people who will see a report; its **readership** (*qv*). It usually appears on the **title page** (*qv*).

Double spacing. Double the usual space between each line of **text** (*qv*). It helps a typist or printer read a manuscript (hand written) report; it makes it easier to correct and amend **drafts** (*qv*); and it can help readers of a report. Other line spacings include 0, ½, 1½, 2½ and 3. Obviously the choice will affect the number of lines on a page.

Draft. An early version of a report drawn up for initial consideration.

Duty notes report. A type of report which explains how a job is to be performed.

End matter. The pages of a report after the **main body** (*qv*) – *cf* **Prelims**.

Enhanced modern format. An **ultra-modern format** (*qv*) of a report with the additional features of added and manipulated images – *cf* **Modern format** and **Traditional format**.

Explanatory report. A type of report which provides a factual account of something that has happened. More specific than an **informative report** (*qv*).

Exploded drawing. A pictorial method of illustrating what something looks like. The components of an object are shown in assembly as if they were spread out along an invisible axis.

Feasibility report. A type of report which discusses the practicality, and possibly the suitability and compatibility of a given project, both in physical and economic terms. It must come to a **conclusion** (*qv*) and must **recommend** (*qv*) that some action is taken or is not taken and/ or that some choice is adopted or is rejected.

Flowchart. A diagrammatic representation of the sequence of operations in a natural, industrial or organisational system.

Font. A set of characters (the alphabet, numbers and symbols) in one weight and style of **typeface** (*qv*).

Footers. Identifying information placed at the bottom of each page of a report – *cf* **Headers**.

Footnote. A note or **reference** (*qv*) placed at the foot of the relevant page; at the end of the relevant section; or towards the end of a report.

Foreword. An introductory section of a report, similar to a **preface** (*qv*) and an **introduction** (*qv*), but usually written by someone other than the author of the report.

Format. The general appearance of a report including type style, paper, **binding** (*qv*), covers, **layout** (*qv*), shape and size.

Front matter. See **Prelims**.

Glossary (of Terms) (or **Gloss**). An alphabetical list of unfamiliar difficult, specialised or technical words and phrases, acronyms and abbreviations used in a report.

Gluing. A method of **binding** (*qv*) a report where the sheets are glued and fixed into the spine of a fabric, card or plastic cover.

Go live. To actually undertake a statistical survey (or to operate a system), as distinct from **pilot testing** (*qv*) it.

Graph. A method of presenting figures visually. Particularly useful for illustrating detailed relationships between items or to show a trend over time.

Graphics. Image enhancements, such as lines, boxes and background used to create interesting and appealing visual design.

Harvard referencing. A system for providing **citations** (*qv*) and **references** (*qv*) favoured by many educational institutions.

Headers. Identifying information placed at the top of each page of a report – *cf* **Footers**.

Heading. A means of identifying and labelling a block of **text** (*qv*). It should be specific; comparatively short; expected, or at least easily interpreted; and should cover all the ground collectively. It should be more prominent than a **subheading** (*qv*), but less prominent than the **title** (*qv*). Headings of similar rank should introduce topics of roughly equal importance.

Highlighting. Drawing attention to important parts of the **text** (*qv*) by methods other than **headings** (*qv*) e.g. using upper case or changing **spacing** (*qv*).

House-style. A consistent style of report writing developed by and used within an organisation.

Illustration. A pictorial representation of information as distinct from **text** (*qv*). Every illustration should have a **caption** (*qv*) and figure number and must be referred to in the text. If there are more than just one or two illustrations, they should be listed separately on the **contents page** (*qv*).

Indentation. A method of refining the appearance of **text** (*qv*) where the beginning of a line is inset a number of spaces to indicate a new paragraph; for emphasis; or to break up a large passage.

Index. An alphabetical list of items discussed in a report together with their page and/or paragraph numbers. An index should contain more entries than a **contents page** (*qv*). Necessary only in a large report.

Indexing. A method of improving the presentation of a report and a way of helping readers find their way around it. The various sections or subsections are separated and distinguished, perhaps by means of overlapping pages or protruding self-adhesive labels.

Informative report. A type of report which increases the readers' knowledge of an event or brings them up to date. More general than an **explanatory report** (*qv*).

Instructional manual. A type of report which explains how a process (a specific series of actions that bring about a specific result) is to be performed – *cf* **Process description report**.

Internet. The most famous computer **network** (*qv*) which connects thousands of smaller networks and millions of users all around the world.

Interview report. A type of report which forms the framework of an interview (although it must not dictate it), and which records facts and opinions about a candidate in a consistent format to facilitate subsequent evaluation and comparison with other candidates.

In-text referencing. See *Citations*.

Introduction. A section of a report which sets the scene. It states the author's intentions – **the terms of reference** (*qv*) – and gives the **aims** (*qv*) and **scope** (*qv*) of the report. An introduction must include everything the readers will need to know before they read the rest of the report.

Investigation into the financial affairs of a company report. A type of report concerned with some specific aspect of a company's financial affairs as defined by the **terms of reference** (*qv*) and/or by statutory regulations.

Isometric drawing. A pictorial method of illustrating what something looks like. Easy to draw but the lack of perspective makes the object look peculiar.

Justification. A method of refining the appearance of **text** (*qv*) where both the left and the right-hand edges are straight.

KISS. Stands for **K**eep **I**t **S**hort and **S**imple. A very useful principle in all aspects and in all stages of report writing.

Landscape. A page **orientation** (*qv*) where printing is aligned horizontally on the long edge of the paper – *cf* **portrait**.

Layout. The arrangement of **illustrations** (*qv*) and **text** (*qv*).

Leading question. A question phrased so as to suggest the answer expected. In **statistical sampling** (*qv*) it leads to a **bias** (*qv*) in the results obtained. Therefore it must be avoided.

Legend. See **Caption**.

Libel. A false statement of a defamatory nature about another person that tends to damage his or her reputation and which is presented in a permanent form, such as in writing.

Logical substructure. A **substructure** (*qv*) where procedures or events are discussed in the *sequence* in which they occur or occurred.

Lower case. Non-capital letters – *cf* **Upper case**.

Main body. The section of a report which contains the main discussion on the subject-matter as defined by the **terms of reference** (*qv*).

Minutes. A type of report which provides a record of business transacted at a meeting. It may well have some legal and authoritative force.

Modern format. A report which takes advantage of the ability to add lines and boxes, change **font size** (*qv*) and use italics. Otherwise it is basically like a **traditional format** (*qv*) – *cf* **Enhanced modern format** and **Ultra-modern format**.

Network. A collection of telecommunications equipment and transmission lines, used to interconnect devices, such as computers, at different locations so they can exchange information.

Numbering system. A method of identifying the various components of a report for reference and **indexing** (*qv*) purposes. Keep it simple.

Organisational chart. A diagram which depicts the hierarchy of, and the lines of command within, an organisation.

Orientation. Whether the print of a report is aligned horizontally on the long edge (**landscape**, *qv*) or vertically on the short edge (**portrait**, *qv*) of the paper.

Orthographic drawing. A pictorial method of illustrating something. It shows the back, front and side elevations of an object. Of little use where the reader needs to know what it actually looks like.

Pareto principle. 80% of what is important is represented by 20% of what exists. Not to be taken literally, but a very useful general concept to consider during all stages of report writing.

Patterned notes. A method of note taking based on the formation of visual links between facts and ideas, both already known and to be discovered. A very useful way of planning a report, as distinct from writing it – *cf* **Traditional notes**.

Perspective drawing. A pictorial method of illustrating what something looks like. It shows what an object actually looks like. Often difficult to draw.

Pictogram. A method of presenting figures visually by the use of symbols. Very useful for illustrating relationships between items.

Pie chart. A method of presenting figures visually. Very useful for illustrating relative proportions – or how the total pie is divided up.

Pilot test. An initial test of a **questionnaire** (*qv*) or other statistical device among a small number of **respondents** (*qv*) (or an initial test of a new system) to highlight any obvious errors, omissions, ambiguities or other shortcomings before it **goes live** (*qv*).

Plastic gripper. A method of **binding** (*qv*) a report by placing a plastic slide grip along the left hand edge of the assembled covers and sheets.

Population. The total number of people or items within a defined group.

Portrait. A page **orientation** (*qv*) where printing is aligned vertically on the short edge of the paper – *cf* **Landscape**.

Preface. An introductory section to a report. Often used to convey some *personal* background details behind the production of a report.

Prelims (or **Preliminaries**, or **Front matter**). The pages of a report before the **main body** (*qv*) – *cf* **End matter**.

Probability theory. A statistical concept concerned with the effects of chance on an event, experiment, or observation. The basis of **statistical sampling** (*qv*).

Process description report. A type of report which helps readers understand a process (a specific series of actions that bring about a specific result) – *cf* **Instructional manual**.

Progress report. A type of report which describes how some activity or process is advancing.

Proofreading. Checking and making corrections on a document prepared by a typist or printer. It is very important to identify and correct spelling mistakes and errors and inconsistencies in layout before a report is reproduced and issued.

Questionnaire. A method of gathering information by questioning **respondents** (*qv*).

Quota sampling. A method of **statistical sampling** (*qv*) used to obtain a *balanced* view from people based on their sex, age and possibly social class. However, *within* every defined group or population (e.g. Females, aged 21–30; or Males, aged 41–50), the sample is random.

Random sample. In **statistical sampling** (*qv*), each member of the population has an equal chance of being selected.

Readership. The people who will read a report, as listed on the **distribution list** (*qv*). The report is written for them so they must be given the information they need and in a form that they can understand without undue effort.

Recommendations. A section of a report where the author states what specific actions should be taken, and by whom and why, given the **terms of reference** (*qv*), the findings as presented in the **main body** (*qv*), and the **conclusions** (*qv*) reached. Recommendations therefore must look to the future and should always be realistic. Do not make them unless they are required by the terms of reference.

Reference number. A unique number allocated to a report. It should appear on the **title page** (*qv*).

References. A section of a report which provides full details of publications mentioned in the **text** (*qv*), or from which extracts have been quoted – *cf* **Bibliography** and **Citations** and **Resources**.

Report. A document produced to convey information to a specific audience at a certain moment in time.

Research report. A type of report which extends our understanding of the world by reducing our uncertainty and increasing our comprehension of it.

Resources. An alternative name for **Bibliography** (*qv*). Technically, the correct name for the section listing of every **source** (*qv*) given **citations** (*qv*) in the **text** (*qv*), not merely books and other written material. *cf* **Footnote** and **Harvard referencing** and **References**.

Respondent. A person who answers questions, perhaps posed in the form of a **questionnaire** (*qv*).

Ring binding. A method of **binding** (*qv*) a report where a special machine perforates the binding edge and then threads the binding through the holes in the covers and the report. Looks very professional.

Saddle stitching. A method of **binding** (*qv*) a report by means of thread or wire through the fold. See **Stitching**.

Sampling. See *Statistical sampling*.

Scientific report. A type of report which gives an account of a test or experiment together with findings and **conclusions** (*qv*).

Scope. A statement of what was done, and perhaps what was not done – and why it was not done – if the readers could reasonably have assumed that it would have been. It may also include discussion on the resources available to and utilised by the report writer; the **sources of information** (*qv*); the working methods employed; and the **structure** (*qv*) of the report. It usually appears in the **introduction** (*qv*).

Sectional substructure. A **substructure** (*qv*) where information is presented in meaningful sections, e.g. the work of each department in turn or each engineering or clerical function in turn.

Simple random sampling. A method of **statistical sampling** (*qv*) where every person or item in a population has an equal chance of being selected, e.g. take ten names out of a hat.

Skeletal framework. An initial overall plan of the **structure** (*qv*) of a report. A well-planned skeletal framework is the key to effective report writing. It may be revised at any stage(s) during the preparation of the report.

Source (of information). Any person, book, organisation etc supplying information or evidence (specially of an original or primary character) used in a report.

Spacing. See **Double spacing**.

SQ3R. A method of reading. Stands for **S**urvey, **Q**uestion, **R**ead, **R**ecall, **R**eview. The way you read should vary according to the complexity of the material and the reasons for reading it.

Statistical sampling. A method of drawing conclusions about a population by testing a representative sample of it. It is based on **probability theory** (*qv*). See **Quota sampling; Simple random sampling; and Systematic random sampling**.

Stitching. A method of **binding** (*qv*) a report where sheets are folded in the middle to make two single-sided or four double-sided pages, and are then bound by **saddle stitching** (*qv*).

Structure. The arrangement of the components which collectively make up a report.

Subheading. A means of more specifically and precisely identifying and labelling a block of **text** (*qv*) which comes under an overall **heading** (*qv*). Do not use too many subheadings; if necessary re-structure the report to have more headings. Make the subheadings less prominent.

Substructure. The arrangement of material within each of the components of a report, although often applied specifically to the **main body** (*qv*). See **Logical substructure; Sectional substructure; and Creative substructure**.

Subtitle. A secondary title expanding the main **title** (*qv*).

Summary. See **Abstract**.

Synopsis. See **Abstract**.

Systems evaluation report. A type of report that evaluates which system out of several alternatives is most suitable for a particular application; or which tests an apparatus or system with a view to possible large scale employment or multiple applications; or which enquires into the causes of failures in an existing operational system. When it serves the last of these purposes, it is sometimes referred to as a **trouble-shooting report** (*qv*).

Systematic diagram. A visual method of illustrating how items within a system are *connected* to one another, eg the map of the London Underground shows how stations are connected.

Systematic random sampling. A method of **statistical sampling** (*qv*) where every person or item in a population has an equal chance of being selected, but the choice is made to a prearranged plan, e.g. every 100th name on the electoral register.

Tally sheet. A sheet used to mark or set down, and later to total, the number of observations of specified items; or to mark or set down, and later to total, the various answers given by all **respondents** (*qv*) to a **questionnaire** (*qv*).

Technical report. A type of report often written at an early stage in a production process.

Technological report. A type of report which is concerned with the application of practical or mechanical sciences in order to achieve a desired aim.

Terms of Reference (T of R). A concise statement of precisely what a report is about. It is essential that these are known/agreed before any work is undertaken and they should be referred to in the **introduction** (*qv*).

Text. The words of a report as distinct from its **illustrations** (*qv*).

Title. The overall **heading** (*qv*) of a report; a restatement of the **terms of reference** (*qv*), but usually using different words. It should be clear, concise, relevant and unique and should be more prominent than any other heading which appears in the report.

Title page. A sheet at the beginning of a report which bears the main title (and **subtitle** [*qv*], where appropriate); the **reference number** (*qv*), the name of the author; and other important information. Every report should have a title page.

Traditional format. A report that used to be produced on a typewriter – *cf* **Enhanced modern format, Modern format** and **Ultra-modern format**.

Traditional notes. A method of note taking where relevant material is condensed using **headings** (*qv*) and **subheadings** (*qv*), with the most important points and arguments being **highlighted** (*qv*). This method is also the basis of report writing, as distinct from report planning – *cf* **Patterned notes**.

Treasury tag. A simple method of **binding** (*qv*) a report. Holes are made in the pages and covers using a punch and then tags are inserted. Useful where amendments and/or inserts such as maps and plans are expected.

Trouble-shooting report. A type of report which locates the cause of some problem, and then suggests ways to remove or treat it. It can deal with people or organisations; or hardware or systems, where it is sometimes referred to as a systems evaluation report (*qv*).

Typeface. A specific type design, such as *Times New Roman* or *Rockwell*.

Typography. The art and style of printing.

Ultra-modern format. A **modern format** (*qv*) of a report with the additional feature of two or more columns – *cf* **Enhanced modern format** and **Traditional format**.

Underline. See **Caption**.

Upper case. Capital letters – *cf* **Lower case**.

Vector. A type of computer image created from lines and shapes – *cf* **Bitmap**.

White space. The empty space on a page.

Word processing. The use of a personal computer system to enter text from a keyboard, import it from a file, or open a 'standard' document and then edit, format, save or print it. As well as offering tools for basic **graphic** (*qv*) embellishments, most word processors allow graphics and tabular information to be imported from other programs – *cf* **Desktop publishing** (**DTP**).

Working papers. Notes recording the detailed information, evidence, findings and **sources** (*qv*) that will form the basis of the **main body** (*qv*), and of any **appendices** (*qv*). Therefore they must be complete and accurate.

Wysiwyg. An acronym meaning *what you see is what you get*. In other words, what you see onscreen is an accurate representation of how the report will print out.

Resources

BOOKS

A good dictionary is an essential tool for any report writer expecting his or her work to be read by others. Chambers, Collins, Longman and Oxford University Press each offer a comprehensive range to suit every need and every pocket.

Butcher's Copy-editing: The Cambridge Handbook, Judith Butcher (Cambridge University Press). An authoritative text used by professional publishers and their editors.

The Complete Plain Words, Sir Ernest Gowers (Penguin). An excellent guide to using plain English and avoiding jargon.

A Dictionary of Modern English Usage, H.W. Fowler, revised by Sir Ernest Gowers (Oxford University Press). A classic guide to English usage, full of fascinating information.

The Handbook of Non-Sexist Writing for Writers, Editors and Speakers, Casey Miller and Kate Swift (Women's Press). The title says it all.

Improving Your Written English, Marion Field (How To Books). Explains the basics of writing good English.

Learn to Draw Charts and Diagrams Step-by-Step, Bruce Robertson (North Light Books). It starts with basic pie charts and ends with sophisticated computer graphic programs.

Mind the Stop, G.V. Carey (Penguin). Everything you ever wanted to know about punctuation.

New Oxford Dictionary for Writers and Editors (Oxford University Press). Provides authoritative advice on 'problem' words and names.

The Oxford Writers' Dictionary, compiled by R.E. Allen (Oxford University Press). Straightforward guidance on problems of grammar, spelling and punctuation.

The Research Book: Internet Research, Andrew Pomeroy (Creative Continuum). A complex topic made clear through detailed explanation.

Roget's Thesaurus. You cannot find a word you have forgotten or do not know in a dictionary. Look up a word of similar meaning in Roget and you will find a variety of words and expressions which should include the one in the back of your mind, or perhaps an unfamiliar one which, when checked in a dictionary, proves even more appropriate. There are many versions available, including a revision by E.M. Kirkpatrick (Longman).

Spring into Technical Writing, Barry J. Rosenberg (Addison Wesley). Helps you communicate technical ideas to any readership.

Titles and Forms of Address – A Guide to Their Correct Use, (A. & C. Black). Getting it right in both formal and informal situations.

The Usborne Guide to Better English, Robyn Gee and Carol Watson (Usborne Publishing). A comprehensive and easy-to-read guide on basic grammar, spelling and punctuation.

Writing Good Reports, John Bowden (How To Books). A handbook which concentrates on the essentials of report writing.

ONLINE

Pages on the Internet are added, removed and revised so rapidly that any extensive listing provided here would soon become obsolete. It is therefore advisable to use a major search engine, such as *Google*, to establish which sites are currently available to you. As the majority will be US-based, you may first need to filter your search in order to focus on styles, approaches and conventions that apply in your own country.

You will find that your results will include many pages that are dedicated to specific fields, such as engineering or accountancy, and to specific users, such as undergraduates or scientists. Do not immediately dismiss them if they do not coincide with your particular background and interests. Much of their advice and instruction is likely to be of value to *all* report writers, not merely to their target audiences.

Three excellent introductions to report writing available at the time of writing are:

http://www.plainenglish.co.uk/reportsguides.pdf
http://www.surrey.ac.uk/skills/pack/report.html
http://unilearning.uow.edu.au/main.html

Index

ه